One Author's Aha Moments

Writing Revelations with a Focus on the Young Adult Market

Jordan Dane

Copyright © 2012 Cosas Finas

All rights reserved. No part of this publication can be reproduced or transmitted in any form or by any means, electronic or mechanical, without permission in writing from the author.

ISBN: 978-0-9855132-0-7

Table of Contents

Introduction 1
   Jordan Dane Bio 2

Chapter 1—I Want to Write a Novel. Where Do I Begin? 3
   Picking a Genre 3
   Write What You Know? 4
   Desire to Write 4
   Are you in it for the Money? 5
   Self-Publishing—A Short Note 6
   Writing Groups or Critique Partners—Are they worth it? 7

Chapter 2—An Overview of Young Adult Fiction 9
   The Cross Genre Young Adult Story 9
   Definitions and Characteristics of Young Adult Fiction 10
   The Ever-Changing and Dynamic Face of Young Adult Fiction 11
   YA Themes 13
   The Voice of YA 14

Chapter 3—How to Create Characters Editors Are Looking For 20
   Conflict is Key 20
   Will there be Romance? 21
   Where to Get Ideas for Characters or Plot 22

The "What If" Question 24
Five Key Ways to Make Your Character Memorable 25
Anti-Heroes, Anti-Heroines and Villains Need
   Love Too—Twelve Tips 28
Getting to Know the Characters You Create 31
The Defining Scene—How to Introduce Your
   Main Character 33
Channeling Your Character—Free Association
   Method 36
Point of View—Wicked Good POV Can Get
   Your Freak On 39
Writing for a Series—Creating a Character and
   World to go the Distance 44

Chapter 4—Plot Structure—An Overview 47
Author's Bucket List on Plot Structure—For
   "Pantsers" or Plotters 48
9-Act Screenplay Structure—Plotting Resource 50
Word of Caution: Pitfalls of Using a Formula 52

Chapter 5—Pacing Your Novel 54
Create a Page Turner for Any Genre— Four Tips 54
Thriller Authors Aren't Normal!—Ten Writing
   Tips that Could Make You One of Us 56
The Seduction of Mystery—Make it Work for You 61
Scene Structure for Pacing—Building an
   Onion from the Inside Out 62

Chapter 6—Does Your Book Have a Hook? 65
What is a Hook? 65
How to Define Your Hook 67
Create a Logline 68

Chapter 7—Writer's Life 71
  The Writer's Life, Goal Setting, and Editing 71
  Do You Believe in Writer's Block? 72
  A Word to Teens Who Write 74
  The Reality of Book Promotion 75
  Ten Things I Believe About Writing—A Final Note 78

Dedication 82

Acknowledgments 82

Praise for Jordan Dane 84

Introduction

In my writing career, I've been fortunate to meet many wonderful and generous authors and publishing industry professionals. To repay their many kindnesses, I love the idea of "paying it forward" to others. I've taught many free workshops, both online and in person, and I'm a regular contributor to The Kill Zone blog, the musings of a group of mystery, suspense, and thriller authors. I also belong to a group of fantasy/thriller authors who now write dark Young Adult fiction at Adr3nalin3. On these group blogs, I share my writing epiphanies as I discover them. The links to these blogs are below.

The Kill Zone Blog—http://killzoneauthors.blogspot.com/ (My adult thriller blog)

Adr3nalin3 Blog—http://adr3nalin3.blogspot.com/ (My dark YA blog)

This book is geared toward the aspiring author—with an emphasis on Young Adult fiction—but many of the writing tips will apply to more experienced authors and those of other genres as well. My advice comes from my personal experiences on writing fiction for adult and teen markets and what has worked for me. I don't believe in hard and fast rules when it comes to the creative process, but I sincerely hope to expose you to new ideas that can get you excited about writing.

ONE AUTHOR'S AHA MOMENTS

Jordan Dane—Bio

Avon/HarperCollins launched Jordan Dane's debut suspense novels in a back to back publishing event in the spring of 2008 after the three-book series sold in auction. Ripped from the headlines, Jordan's gritty plots weave a tapestry of vivid settings, intrigue, and dark humor. Publishers Weekly compared her intense pacing to Lisa Jackson, Lisa Gardner, and Tami Hoag—romantic suspense that "crosses over into plain thriller country." Pursuing publication since 2003, this national best selling and critically acclaimed author received awards in 33 national writing competitions. Her debut novel *No One Heard Her Scream* was named Publishers Weekly Best Book of 2008 and Romantic Times Magazine nominated *No One Lives Forever* as Best Intrigue Novel of 2008, with *Evil Without a Face* named as winner of the 2009 National Readers Choice Award. *In the Arms of Stone Angels* (April, 2011, Harlequin Teen) is Dane's first release for young adult, followed by *On a Dark Wing* released in January, 2012. Her next YA books with Harlequin Teen will be a series—*The Hunted*, with release slated for fall 2012 through 2013. Formerly an energy sales manager in the oil and gas industry, she now is following her passion to write full time. Jordan and her husband share their residence with two cats of highborn lineage, two rescue dogs named Taco and Sancho, and the sweet memory of an impossible to forget canine.

For more, visit **www.JordanDane.com**
Or follow JD on Twitter at **https://twitter.com/#!/JordanDane**

Chapter 1

I Want to Write a Novel. Where to Begin?

Picking a Genre

So you want to become an author. What now? Before I began to write, I did research on the publishing industry to see what was selling. Romance is always a big seller—and still is—because women/girls are avid readers, romance can be a big element of what they read, in general. If you look at the stats on romance books posted on the Romance Writers of America website, you'll see that romance is a significant genre as compared to others. The Twilight books by Stephenie Meyer made young romance a popular element in YA too. Romance can be added to any story. It's the new black. It goes with everything.

When most people think about romance, they picture a man and woman in an embrace on the cover, but romance is much more than that. Within the larger umbrella of romance, there are subgenres that provide a lot of options for a writer, including Young Adult (YA) Fiction. Although romance can be an element added to YA, there are so many other story elements you can write. For a new author, I recommend looking at your favorite reads to see what elements you have enjoyed. If you are an avid reader, chasing someone else's trend doesn't make sense. If you buy enough books and read what you love, then you *are* a valid market to target. Write a book that you want to read. If the story strikes a chord with you, it will for someone else too.

Reading is a great way to discover what you want to write. Read, read, read then read some more. Look at what's on your bookshelf now. What are your favorite kinds of books? Writing the kind of book you've always loved is a good first step. If you want to write for the young adult market, read it. Lots of it.

But simply because you might want to write it doesn't mean romantic elements will come easy. Emotional storytelling is far from simple. In YA, you have to tap into that first innocent crush, awkward flirtations, the thrill of being kissed for the first time, the agony of being rejected or the betrayal of being taken advantage of—and do it with raging hormones under peer pressure. In YA, love is experimentation too. How honestly will you portray that? How much of your own experiences will you filter in?

In the end, I think the most successful first book is one you write from your heart. You'll write a novel that you're more passionate about.

Write What You Know?
A piece of advice you will hear when you first start out is the phrase "write what you know," but I think it should be "write what you fear…what you love…what you hate." Writing what you know is too limiting. That's where solid research comes in, but writing about emotion is something we all can do. Conveying emotion in our writing will resonate with readers and only you can tell a story filtered through your life's experiences.

Desire to Write
I heard a motivational speaker say that he wrote his non-fiction book doing it a page a day. That was a glaring light bulb that went off in my head. It lit the dark corners of my mind, reviving my

desire or passion for writing, a dream I've had since I was a teenager. Ever since I heard those words, I found time to write a little every day. And after countless rejections from agents and editors—*countless*—I had come to my crossroad. I had to ask myself—if I never sold, would I still write every day? When my answer was 'hell, yeah,' I knew that writing had become the air that I breathed. It was a quality of life thing. I simply *had* to write.

How many people do you know feel that strongly about *anything*? Once I knew that I had made a lifetime commitment to write, whether I sold or not, that's when I got the attention of New York City. My "first sale" story is on my website at *www.JordanDane.com* (on my adult book site '*For Writers*' page). So many things contributed to how I got published—I even sacrificed a body part—but one international bestselling author stuck her neck out and helped me most. Teaching workshops, speaking at author meetings, and writing this book are ways I "pay it forward."

Are you in it for the money?

If lightning strikes and you sell, what kind of advance can you expect? I don't mean to sound negative, but in this economy, it's tougher than ever to get published by a big house that can market and distribute your book. Lowering your expectations (of what getting published means) might help you hunker down into more realistic goals. That way you can spew coffee out of your nose when you get 'the call' from New York and find out you've hit the publishing lotto.

If you get any money at all, most authors earn a typical advance against royalties ranging from $1,500-5,000 per novel for a single-title book (a long enough story to not be considered a novella or short story. See publisher's guidelines for submission lengths). Writing is generally nothing to quit your day job over. Even if you sell big, you must be ready to financially weather the storm of a fickle publishing industry.

ONE AUTHOR'S AHA MOMENTS

I had financial goals already in place with years of income squirreled away for both my husband and I before I retired from my lucrative day job in the energy industry to write full time. When you hear the words "Don't quit your day job"—that's good advice unless you've done a lot of planning. Ultimately, you really have to want to publish for the sheer joy of holding your book in your hands and knowing others will read your baby. Few authors get to write full time without other financial support to back them up.

Self-Publishing—A Short Note

Many authors give up on getting published by a traditional publishing house and end up self-publishing. Don't get caught up with a scam that could bilk you out of thousands of dollars. Amazon, Barnes and Noble, Smashwords, and Kobe, for example, have self-publishing companies now that can sell your book online, but YOU still have to sell it or promote it. From what I've seen, if you have a marketing platform in place and work the social media to get noticed, it generally takes a few books to develop a name if you don't already have one. Be prepared to work at the business of writing, as well as creating new books, to build on your momentum. However, I'm excited about the potential in publishing today.

The self-publishing arena isn't easy, but it can get you noticed by traditional publishers through a solid performance. It can also be fulfilling to see readers enjoying your book while getting paid for it. Very cool. Because these companies deal in digital sales, the units sold are reported more immediately and are easily documented so they can offer monthly or quarterly sales payments, which is a great cash flow improvement over traditional publishers with their six-month royalty period statements. (With reporting delays, this could translate to a once a year statement and no guarantee on receiving any money at all if an author is working off an advance on royalty.) Traditional publishing houses also retain funds against returned books, so your cash flow can be affected by this too.

This is a huge topic and I won't cover it much here, but as I've said, there is so much potential in publishing today and this is one of those areas that can pay off if you have the goods. Don't give up on your dream to traditionally publish if you really want to do it, but once you decide to try it on your own, there are services that can help you bundle your book for loading and distributing online. You can also do many of these things yourself to keep your fixed cost down, like learning how to format your own book.

To set your book apart from countless others, I would focus on the quality of your fiction writing, the editing/copy editing, and the cover. What hurts most first timers' efforts is poor writing, a book riddled with typos and grammar errors, and a cheap-looking cover they designed on their own. They rush to get their book out before it is polished, then find they have a steeper uphill to climb in order to build a following on a shaky foundation. In my opinion, there is no shortcut to creating a good fiction book. Good writing should be foremost in an author's mind.

Writing Groups and Critique Partners—Are They Worth it?

If you live in a big city, you might be lucky enough to join several writing groups. Look for an active group that offers programs in author craft, research topics, and maybe promotional support once you've sold. Getting exposed to craft concepts and networking with other authors can be invaluable when you are first starting out, but remember that writing is still primarily a solitary sport.

Everyone will feel obliged to offer advice on your book. Heed what fits and don't be afraid to reject what doesn't. Too many people reading and critiquing your work can dilute your voice. Self-doubt can also wear down your confidence. You need to maintain a strong sense of who you are as a writer. Listen to feedback, be grateful to those who take the time to share their solicited advice, but make only those changes that seem logical to you. It's your story. You are the final judge of what stays and what goes. You're in control. It's your book.

When you first start out, it's important to commiserate with other writers. You learn a lot and fast. I had critique groups that I'd started or participated in, but eventually I dropped out. A group can be work too. It's great when someone reads your stories, but this is usually a two-way street. You have to read theirs too. If your group is too large, you can get bogged down by other people's work. Invariably, some group members write faster than others and it's easy to get tied up in other authors' careers rather than your own.

Critique partners (beta readers) have things that they each do well, but most will line edit you. They can spell check and wordsmith you to death. After a while, I didn't get much out of that. I wanted someone to read for the big picture of character motivation and higher level plot views and scene selection choices. People who can critique like this are hard to come by. If you find one, grab hold of them and treat them well. They're worth their weight in gold. I tend to like working one-on-one with writers like this or I work with a select few where each one offers something special that I may need. For example, some people are great at writing with emotion while others might have an effective critical eye for action scenes.

Once I got published by a traditional publisher, I found I didn't have much time to have someone "beta read" for me. Deadlines got in the way, but I love the camaraderie and the friendship that a local group of authors can provide. In the end, though, it's all about you applying your butt to the seat and writing.

Chapter 2

An Overview of Young Adult Fiction

The true beauty of Young Adult (YA) Fiction is that it defies the traditional adult book with its cross genre imagination and world building. YA is only limited by the author's creative juices. So before I try to characterize YA, I want to share a word of caution. What I will share in this book is only a starting point to define what YA can be, but these are not hard and fast rules that should create borders in your mind. I hate rules. Consider these as guideposts, but don't let my thoughts limit how you see YA. Strive to be the trendsetter. Create a new subgenre. We all have that ability.

The Cross Genre Young Adult Story
I'd like to make a point about the cross genre book. The publishing industry works hard at categorizing types of books to make it easier for booksellers to classify the book and shelve it for the reading public. As authors keeping up with trends, we learn the subgenre lingo, but some books defy a strict definition because they have many elements to them. Young adult novels are a great example of cross genre story telling. Most have multiple genre elements combined and it all works. The only limitation to a YA book is the author's imagination. Whether your book idea is pure fantasy, urban fiction, edgy YA, or YA romance, YA is hot for new authors with ideas. It's a growing trend that publishing houses are buying. Now it's time for you as an author to learn your craft and create

a book that the industry is already primed to buy. What will you write?

Definition and Characteristics of Young Adult Fiction

1. YA fiction, whether in the form of novels or short stories, has distinct attributes that distinguish it from the other age categories of fiction: Adult fiction (18 yrs+), Middle Grade or Tween Fiction (ages 10-12), and Children's Fiction (under 10 yrs).

2. Targets boys and girls, ages 12-18.

3. The vast majority of YA stories portray an adolescent as the central protagonist, rather than an adult or a child.

4. YA books have other unique traits, such as voice, style, and theme that make it more complex. An author can't simply put a teen protagonist into a plot geared for adults. The mentality and experience level of the protagonist must be age-appropriate.

5. The subject matter and story lines are typically consistent with the age and experience of the main character, but beyond that YA stories span the entire spectrum of fiction genres. (As an avid reader of YA, I personally love the cross genre storylines. I write this way for my adult books too. Again, I encourage authors to write the stories that they want to read.)

6. The tone, style, and content of a YA novel changes depending on the specific age of the target audience.

7. YA can tackle G-rated issues or it can be very edgy. "Edgy" YA tackles controversial or difficult topics, such as teen suicide, rape, or drug abuse.

8. The settings of YA stories are limited only by the imagination and skill of the author. (This is another cool thing about YA. It stretches your imagination as an author, even if you write for other genres.)

9. Themes in YA stories often focus on teen challenges. These books are sometimes referred to as "problem novels" or "coming of age" novels. (No matter what my plot is, there are always underlying themes that can change the storyline and add to the conflicts within a character's story arc. That emotional subplot can add depth and make your book great.)

10. Writing styles of YA stories range widely, from the richness of literary style to the simple clarity and speed of free verse. (Most true lovers of YA are very eclectic and read very diverse books. If you don't feel comfortable writing in a certain style, try another way to tell your story.)

11. YA books share the fundamental elements of fiction with other stories: character, plot, setting, theme, and style. It's important to learn the craft of writing. Even if you plan to break the rules, understand them first. (Don't ever settle for how you write now. Strive for making your NEXT BOOK your best one. Be a sponge for learning your craft.)

12. Generally, YA books run between 40,000 and 75,000 words, depending on the target age group, but they certainly can go longer. (Mine range from 80,000 words and that's in my contract too, but this can vary house to house.)

The Ever-Changing and Dynamic Face of Young Adult Fiction

YA subgenres mirror that of adult books. For example, subgenres can include urban fantasy, fantasy, romance, mystery, sci-fi, historical, suspense, paranormal, and thrillers, but how YA differs in bookstores is that these books are typically shelved under the larger umbrella of Teen Fiction in one location, rather than being shelved by subgenre. When adult books are categorized by subgenres, it can sometimes make it tough for an author's book to be found in stores. The reading public might expect an author under the mystery section, but the books are being promoted by the publisher as romantic suspense. For the most part, I like the fact that YA books are lumped together. Teens can browse book aisles without having to understand how books are being promoted or shelved.

The category of YA fiction continues to expand into new forms and subgenres: e-books, graphic novels (modern comics with terrific art), light novels or novellas, Manga (a Japanese version of graphic novels), even subcategories such as cyberpunk, splatterpunk, techno-thrillers, and contemporary Christian fiction.

Below are clarifications for the more unique subgenres I mentioned.

- **Cyberpunk**—A science fiction dystopian genre noted for its focus on "high tech" and "low life." Conflicts often center on a conflict among hackers, artificial intelligence, and mega-corporations and tend to be in a near future Earth.
- **Splatterpunk**—Horror fiction that is graphic, often gory, and a depiction of violence with no limits—a revolt against the more traditional horror story.
- **Steampunk**—A tongue in cheek variant of Cyberpunk and a sub-genre of Sci-Fi, fantasy, or alternative history that can involve a setting where steam power is still widely used (usually Victorian era Britain or the Wild West era), usually inspired from Sci-Fi stories in the vein of Jules Verne and H G Wells. You'll see variations of this basic definition.
- **Techno-thrillers**—A hybrid genre, these books draw on spy

thrillers, war novels, and sci-fi, but use a disproportionate amount of technical detail.

YA Themes

I've included a list of themes below and hope they help generate ideas for your book, but don't sweat over your theme, especially if it keeps you from writing the book. If you "pick" a theme beforehand—and you're not careful—you can force your writing to hit readers over the head with your "lesson" or theme. That's one of the reasons I don't make a big deal about themes until the process becomes a mental exercise after the fact or I find certain character motivations compelling as I'm writing each scene. I want my story to be what it is—organically—without contrivance or a life's lesson to be learned. Some authors, however, really like the idea of writing for a theme. If that inspires you, then go for it.

Some YA Themes
  Abuse, Sexual Violence, and Healing
  Accepting Difference
  Accidents and Adjustments
  Addressing Addiction
  Animals' and the Environment's Importance in our Lives
  Beauty's Meaning
  Breaking Silence, Speaking Out
  Crime and Suicide and Their Aftermath
  Dating Challenges
  Disease and Disability
  Emotional Problems Confronted
  Families, Traditional and Redefined
  Friends Forever?
  Guilty or Innocent?
  Heroes: What Does It Mean To Be a Hero?
  History Is About Young Adults, Too
  Imagined Futures
  Imagined Places

Insiders and Outsiders
Jobs: Taking Adult Responsibility
Old Tales Retold: Fairy Tales, Legends, Myths
Older People's Impact on our Lives
Parents' Absence, Parents' Presence
Pregnancy, Parenthood, Abortion
Poverty's Challenges
Religion and Spiritual Life
School Days
Sexual Identity, Sexual Desire
Supernatural and Alien Beings: Confronting the Other
Survival
Teammates
War's Impact

The Voice of YA

In preparation for researching YA voice, I looked through my volumes of YA books, looking for examples of voice. If you're unfamiliar with YA, you might expect to find contemporary pop culture references, witty snarky banter, and prose most adults might need subtitles to understand as examples of "teen speak," but YA voice is much more than that.

As many kinds of teens there are, that's how many varied "voices" you can create. As long as the story is compelling and the characters draw in the reader, the voice of YA only needs to match the tone, age, and character of that story. Don't force voice or language that doesn't seem real to you. Your protagonist's voice should come naturally from the story premise and the conflict, filtered through your head as the author. If you force it, it will show.

I've read clever teen speak before and chuckled with the humor, but when it came time to write my own first YA book—*In the Arms of Stone Angels* (Harlequin Teen)—I wanted my story to be about kids I saw in the region (Oklahoma and Texas), or my nieces and nephews. I was more concerned with making Brenna Nash read like a real kid who had been put in a terrible situation that made her what she was. Her ordeal (and its aftermath) affected her. During a time when most kids are discovering who they are, Brenna's life had stopped the day this 14-year old witnessed a horrendous murder and saw who knelt by the body, covered in blood. That day her life became an uphill struggle. The concept of "arrested development" took over where she would remain stuck at fourteen, trapped in that terrible moment in her life. I relied on my gut instincts to create her and her voice.

Also, in order for the reader to believe she is in a horrible place emotionally, I couldn't let outward sarcasm rule her voice. She had more internal dialogue because she was afraid of speaking out or was used to being alone. If your teen is in real trouble and you're writing suspense, too much sarcasm or humor can ruin the threat you're trying to portray.

If you're trying to write a kick-ass heroine, she might have an "attitude" and a specific voice, but if you expect the reader to worry for her, you should consider making her vulnerable and justifiably afraid when it counts. To me, it's more important to comprehend the psychology of a kid who is faced with the terrible things you are writing about. Good stories are based on real emotion.

Below are things I learned about YA voice:
- **Use First Person or Deep Point of View (POV)**—This technique of "deep" POV, or "close third" person, is used in fiction writing as a glimpse into the head of your character. In YA, I think of deep POV or close third as conversational thoughts deep inside your teen. First person POV is like reading someone's diary. (See more on how to accomplish this in Chapter 3—Channeling Your Character—Free Association Method.)

- **Don't be afraid to mix POVs**—You can mix POVs (for example, first person for your storyteller and third person for other characters), but since it's your story, only you can decide how you want it to be told. Many YA stories are in first person, but more authors are exploring a mix. By adding in the element of third person for other characters, you can let the reader in on what is happening outside your character's head and add twists to your plot more effectively. Plus if you have secondary characters or villains who may threaten your protagonist, letting the reader in on what's in their head can make the reader more fearful for your hero/heroine. (I also think mixing POVs is a good transition for kids when they're ready for adult books. Most adult books are not in first POV, but first POV is very intimate and fun to write.)

- **Don't worry about your vocabulary**—Today's teen reader can handle it. There's no need to simplify your choice of words or sentence structure if the character warrants it. Just be mindful of the experience level and education of the teen in your story. A homeless kid without much education won't have an extensive vocabulary unless there's a good reason for it. If you're writing a futuristic dystopian book, you'll be world building and perhaps coming up with your own vocabulary or teen life choices or social customs that would be different from a contemporary YA.

- **Character first or story first?** In my adult fiction thrillers, characters usually come at me first, but in YA I think it's important to conceive a plot then fit the best characters to the premise. This may help you conjure the most fitting character and voice for the story.

- **How does the story and character motivation affect your storyteller's voice?** One of the biggest mistakes writers make in YA usually has to do with the sarcastic voice. Biting sarcasm alone does not make a YA story. Without a reason for this behavior, the author runs the risk of making their character unbearable, unlikeable and a real turnoff for the reader. The manuscript must have a cohesive story with solid character motivation to go along with the attitude. Even if the voice is great, what happens? Something needs to happen. And if your character starts off with a good reason to be snarky, give them a journey that will change them by the end of the book.

- **Know your character's motivation**—Sarcasm, voice, and maturity of your character must be driven by a reason in your story to add depth. Provide a foundation for the "attitude" your character has and don't forget a liberal dose of poignancy. A reader can tolerate a sarcastic teen if a scene ends with brutal honesty or catches the reader off guard with something gripping to make the whole thing come to a real point.

- **Beware of stereotypes**—Avoid the cliché character (the geeky nerd, the pretty cheerleader, the dumb jock). This doesn't only apply to YA.

- **Can you relate to your storyteller?** Peer pressure, dating, zits, kissing, sex, being an outsider, not fitting in—these are teen concerns that, as adults, we have to remind ourselves about. With each of these words, what pops into your head? Does it trigger a memory, good or bad? Sometimes the best scenes can come from these universal concerns that haven't changed for decades. Filtered through your own experiences, a scene can carry more weight if it's still relevant and relatable.

ONE AUTHOR'S AHA MOMENTS

- **What is your storyteller like emotionally?** What effect can raging hormones do for your character? Is everything a drama? Not all teens are like this. Some are withdrawn in front of adults or in social situations. It's important to ask yourself: What are they like around their friends and who are their friends? I would resist the urge to create a character based on a teen you know if it's at the expense of your plot. Certain aspects or perceptions of "your teen" can influence your character, but your book is fiction. That's why I recommend devising your plot first before you place the right teen in it.

- **Who or what has influenced your storyteller most?** Like in the movie, *JUNO*, the teen girl had a dry wit that sometimes referenced an older person's humor. Not everything was "teen speak." She was influenced by the adults in her life, using references she heard from her dad and step-mom. Her pop culture references were peppered into the humor of another generation. She still sounded young, but her dialogue appeal was more universal.

- **What journey will your storyteller take in your book?** Getting the voice right is only half the challenge. Your YA book must be about something—a plot, believable world building, and the reaction and journey of a real teen amidst it all.

- **Don't forget the imagery**—Teen readers have great imaginations and can picture things in their heads like a movie. Give them something that triggers and engages their imaginations. Picture your book scenes on the big screen and write them that way, but don't go overboard and slow your pace. Teens get it. Give them a glimpse and move on. They'll roll with the imagery.

- **Turn off your parent switch**—If you're an adult and a parent writing YA, you may find it difficult to turn off your mother or father switch, but you should consider it. Kids can read between the lines if you're trying too hard to send them a "universal parental" message about conduct and behavior. Simply focus on your story and tap into what your teen experiences were—without censorship—and without the undertone of sending kids a special message. Your story will read as more honest, without an ulterior motive.

Chapter 3

How to Create YA Characters Editors Are Looking For

Characters can come at you from any direction. You can spot them in a grocery store, or (heaven forbid) at a family reunion, or they can whisper to you in your dreams in the middle of the night. (A little creepy, right?) Only you will recognize them, to know if they'll stick in your head and make the cut for a book. Below are some thoughts on creating characters, things that I've learned from my own writing. An integral part of character building is conflict. No matter how compelling your character might be to you, if you don't 'test' your character with a challenging conflict, you don't have a compelling enough story.

Conflict is Key

What does your character want and why can't they have it? Conflict is vital to creating memorable characters. No conflict(s), no story. I can't emphasize this enough. If there is a common mistake many aspiring authors make, it's not having enough conflict to keep a story flowing through to the end that will drive the characters and keep their story interesting.

Your external conflict might be the villain or the insurmountable situation, but the most unforgettable characters will also contend with their own flaws or biases (internal conflicts) or demons, so they have a journey toward self-discovery. If you have a hero who is in conflict with a villain, while he's battling his own demons, then think about creating a heroine who has opposing conflicts where one of them must lose in order to be together. Conflicts are best when layered. (See more in Chapter 5 on Pacing Your Novel.)

Find your characters' greatest weaknesses or fears—their internal conflicts—and demand they deal with it. Torture them. It's legal. Rubbing their nose in it generally comes from the influences of the external conflict—the plot. The one-two punch of the external and internal conflicts adds depth to your character. Make him/her suffer, then ramp up the stakes and the tension. It's all about drama!

Will there be Romance?

Will there be a young budding romance in your book? If you're a savvy author, aware that most readers are female, you might want to consider an element of romance in your YA story. So what's the right balance of romance to the overall plot? If you can take the romance out of your book—completely delete the flirting intimacy and growing attraction between your boy and girl—and your book no longer makes sense, that's when you know you have the right blend.

If you have a completely separate story arc for just the relationship development and it's not an integral part of the plot, then you haven't blended the romance in well enough. You have to punish your characters for wanting to be together. Put them in more danger or make them more vulnerable because they have feelings for one another. Ramp up the stakes. Remember, as an author, it's your job to torture them, and it's legal.

Many YA books feature a love triangle. In a teen girl's life, it's conceivable that she could have more than one boy vying for her attention. But this theme seems to be a contrived formula these days, and teens notice if you don't have a good enough foundation for the triangle.

ONE AUTHOR'S AHA MOMENTS

In my book—*On a Dark Wing*—I have a strange combination of boys who have my girl's attention. One boy is her best friend, a boy in a wheelchair. Another is a fantasy of hers, a guy who doesn't even know she exists, and the final boy is not a boy at all. He's not human. The ending is bittersweet, but I made sure that she learned something about love, loyalty, and sacrifice in the process. I never hit readers over the head with a theme. I prefer to let them make their own conclusions.

In *Indigo Awakening* (Book #1 in my "*The Hunted*" series for Harlequin Teen)—I have another strange triangle. One psychic boy is mentally linked to a girl who is older than he is, but the mind link to him is like making love for the first time. It changes everything for both of them. Since this boy is evolving into the next evolution of mankind, this girl is motivated to be with him so she can be a part of a new movement. Boy #2 has a secret crush on the same girl, but he's driven more by protecting a young homeless boy—a conflict that will drive how he feels for this girl. Jealousy will play a part on his side of the equation, but he's more influenced by protecting the home he built for this kid he wants to protect. The little boy's life is on the line if boy #2 makes the wrong choice of not questioning his loyalty for the girl. The stakes are far greater than boy likes girl. (This goes back to layering the conflict to make a deeper, more emotional story.)

Where to Get Ideas for Characters or Plot

First of all, let's talk about being prepared for lightning to strike. Since book ideas usually come piecemeal, I maintain a file that is fully stuffed with potential story ideas or characters. I also keep pads of paper and pens stashed everywhere in my house, in my car, and definitely in my purse. My husband also got me a digital recorder so I can make quick verbal notes when I'm in the car (not driving, of course). As many of you probably already know firsthand, an author's mind never stops working.

JORDAN DANE

I often thought it would be fun to set up a dartboard with various types of characters, traits, and key plot ideas. I'd toss a dart to see what challenge I could devise for myself. Unfortunately, I can't hit the side of a barn with a Bazooka, but I haven't given up on the notion. I like getting painted into a corner to see how I get out. *Weird, I know.*

I'm sure there are many other ways to conjure ideas, but the following (in no particular order) are where I get some of mine:
- Classic stories or fables
- Real life people that I know personally or see in the news that capture my imagination
- NOVA—the Science Channel
- Cable TV—the weirder the channel, the better
- Newspapers and magazines
- TV and movies
- Any teenager within arm's reach
- Song lyrics—I love songs for inspiration and sometimes create a playlist for books
- Commercials (Women's fiction and mystery author, Marcia Preston, got her idea for *Piano Man* from a sad heart transplant commercial. A beautiful book.)

For my debut YA book, *In the Arms of Stone Angels*, my teen boy came to me first. He didn't have a name yet, but I had seen a strange TV show where an old guy had lightning going off in his head in a psych ward. It made me wonder what it would feel like to be trapped inside your own head, locked in a dark and terrible moment in your life, reliving it in a never-ending loop.

When Susan Johnson, a librarian friend of mine in Oklahoma, contacted me to entice me to write a Native American story set in Oklahoma, she hit me up at the right time while this story was formulating in my head. I called her on the phone and described my boy character as being a half-breed, not fitting in anywhere.

She said, "I know that boy." Susan described how her young friend, White Bird, was a chameleon and changed who he was to fit in. He felt desperate to fit in. I loved his name so much, I asked him if I could use it and he said yes. So there is a real White Bird out there. He's out of the foster care system now and bravely making it on his own and getting his education. A great and smart kid. He helped me research how to make a proper sweat lodge and inspired my teen boy.

For my adult books, characters usually come to me first before I put them into situations that would force them to rise to the occasion. But in YA, I tend to think of a plot idea before I find the best teen to capitalize on the conflict. I do this because I don't want my teen voice to sound the same from book to book. My advice is to listen to that voice you hear in your head. It might be your next book calling…*or schizophrenia*. Either way, don't ignore it. Write your ideas down with your new pen and paper collection.

The "What If" Question
The question "what if" is a powerful one for writers when they are devising plots and characters.
- **What if** blood chemistry is involved in determining who might become a vampyre, not a bite on the neck, and a girl must go to a vampyre "finishing school" or die? (House of Night series by P. C. and Kristin Cast.)
- **What if** a girl was in a tragic car accident that cost her entire family was in a coma, would she want to stay with the living or let go? (*If I Stay* by Gayle Forman)
- **What if** the future of your family, friends, and town—and the very life of your baby sister—depended on you volunteering to fight to the death in a futuristic reality TV show where only one will survive? (*Hunger Games* series by Suzanne Collins)

As you can see from these "what if" scenarios, while the plot is intriguing, it is made even more fascinating when you add a character with a lot to lose. Can you imagine yourself being a kid faced with a life or death scenario you never asked for, when all you want is to go to Prom? Or picture yourself as a kid who has taken her future for granted, only to have everything tragically taken overnight, her family gone. If you were a teen faced with a stark reality, what would you be willing to die for?

Don't just focus all your attention on the good guys or protagonists in your book. Put as much effort into your villains and antagonists and secondary characters too. It will make your book feel more real and build an irresistible conflict.

Formulate an idea of the "big ticket" plot points in your story, including the black moment for your main characters when all seems lost. Then devise who is best to tell that story. (See Chapter 4 on Plotting Structure—An Overview for more on plotting your book.) From your cast of characters (primary and secondary), who will reveal your plot and be your main storyteller? Generally, that would be your protagonist—the person with the most to lose perhaps. I say generally because I don't want to limit you from turning a plot on its ear and telling it from the perspective of the villain, for example. One of my favorite YA books (which I will talk about more later) is *The Book Thief* by Markus Zusak. The narrator is Death, telling the story of a 14-year old girl living during the time of the Holocaust. Death becomes a character. This YA novel is gut-wrenching and beautiful. Truly genius writing.

Five Key Ways to Make Your Characters Memorable

As a fun exercise, watch a memorable movie or TV show and observe the traits of the main characters, the ones you can't take your eyes off of when they're on the big or little screen. What makes them unforgettable? For most of us, it's not the high-octane action that sticks in our heads. It's usually what makes that character human and relatable.

ONE AUTHOR'S AHA MOMENTS

In the TV show *Supernatural*, one of my favorites, the two brothers who are battling demons are more compelling because of the complications the writers of that show heaped on the two young men. The older brother, Dean, can't help but protect his younger brother, Sam. He's protected his brother ever since he was a small boy and Sammie was a baby. (Sam is Dean's source of strength because he's family, but he's also his greatest vulnerability.) When Dean is willing to die and be cursed to an eternity in hell to save his little brother from dying, that motivation comes from more than him being protective. He doesn't think he deserves to be saved. He isn't good enough, smart enough, not like Sam. Sam is worth saving, not him. Dean's internal conflict, his low self-esteem, becomes a major handicap. Sensitive Sammie had the same loyalty beyond reason for his older brother, even though he is battling his addiction to demon blood and a fate that puts him at odds with Dean's fight against demons. He becomes part demon himself—the one thing he never wants to be—but his humanity never wavers. Again, internal and external forces battle inside these young men. The fight goes well beyond demon forces and God's dark angels. Be analytical of TV and movies that you are drawn to, in order to dissect why the characters work for you.

1. **Add Depth to Each Character—Give them a journey**
   - With any journey comes baggage. Be generous. Load on the baggage. Give them a weakness that they'll have to face head-on by the climax of the book.

   - Make them vulnerable by giving them an Achilles Heel. Even the darkest street thug or a fearless young girl with magical powers should have a weakness that may get them killed and certainly makes them more human and relatable.

   - Whether you are writing one book or a series, have a

story arc for your character's journey that spans the series. Will they find peace or love, or some version of a normal life? Will they let someone else into their lives or will they be content to live alone? Will a villain have a chance at redemption? Do what makes sense for your character, but realize that their emotional issues will cloud their judgment and affect how they deal with confrontations. By the end of a book, they should learn something.

2. **Use Character Flaws as Handicaps**
   - Challenge yourself as an author by picking flaws that will make your character stand out and that aren't easy to write about. Sometimes that means you have to dig deep in your own head to imagine things you don't want to think about, but tap into your empathy for another human being. You might surprise yourself.

   - Stay true to the flaws and biases you give your characters. Don't present them to the reader then have the actions of the character contradict those handicaps. Be consistent. If they have strong enough issues, these won't be fixed by the end of the book. Find a way to deal with them.

3. **Clichéd Characters can be Fixed**
   - If you have a clichéd character, you may not need to rewrite your whole story. Try infusing a weird hobby or layer in a unique trait/quality that will set them apart. Maybe the computer nerd writes porn scripts for a local indie film company or the jock writes a secret blog under a girl's name giving advice to teens on love and romance for the local paper. When that hobby is surprising and unexpected, that's what will shine about the character and that's what editors will remember.

4. **Create A Divergent Cast of Characters**
   - Portray your characters in varying degrees of redemption—from the innocent to the "total waste of skin" characters.

   - As in real life, not everyone is good or bad. They are a mix of both.

   - Sometimes it's great to show contrast between your characters by making them do comparable things. How does one character handle his or her love life versus another character?

5. **Flesh Out your Villains or Antagonists**
   - Villains or antagonists are the heroes to their own stories—Spend time getting to know them.

   - Give them goals.

   - Give them a chance at redemption—will they take it?

   - Give them a unique sense of humor or dare to endear them to your reader.

   - The better and more diabolical they are, the more the reader will fear for the safety or well-being of your protagonist.

Anti-Heroes/Heroines and Villains Need Love Too—Twelve Tips

To define what an anti-hero or anti-heroine is, as compared to an outright villain, let me start out by saying that there may not be much difference. (I'm *sort of* kidding.) Anti-heroes/heroines have been popular as antagonists for decades. They are flawed and imperfect and perhaps more relatable than a perfect hero in a white hat.

A good example of a TV anti-hero is Gregory House on the medical drama "House." At times, he is completely unlikeable and the viewer is never quite sure if he's driven to cure people because it's the right thing to do or he simply likes being right. He is fascinating to watch.

I love making a borderline human being into a hero. Writing that type of character can be really challenging. A guy could be dark and brooding, but give him a dog and readers will know instantly that he's worth loving. An outright villain is the obstacle, or protagonist, standing in the way of the anti-hero/heroine. They can have similar complexities to their personalities, but they are clearly "bad guys or girls." As an author, you control how much bad and good ends up in their nature.

Below are other tips to add depth to your villain or make your anti-hero/heroine more sympathetic.

1. **Give Them a Reason**—A reader will lose interest pronto if your character is a complete jerk wad for half the book. Sprinkle in the valid reasons for them being who they are and clue the reader in on these reasons early so they can buy in, even if the other characters don't know their motivations.

2. **Does Gender Make a Difference**? In general, I've noticed that readers accept bad boys faster than they embrace a female lead character who isn't perfect. I don't know why this is. Maybe it's the way women or girl readers are about other females. This makes crafting your female characters important.

ONE AUTHOR'S AHA MOMENTS

3. **Make them human**—Give them a code they live by or loyalties a reader can understand and empathize with. Even a dastardly villain or dark anti-hero/heroine has a softer side. In *Silence of the Lambs*, Hannibal Lecter was Clarice's protector with his peculiar brand of loyalty. It was his one endearing trait, that and his culinary skills with liver. Chianti and fava beans, anyone?

4. **Give Them a Soft Edge**—If you give even the toughest brooding character a pet or a soft spot for a kid, they will be endearing to readers. Write the darkest character and match them up with something soft and you've got a winning combination.

5. **Show Respect**—Everyone looks up to a good leader. Show that others admire or respect your dark character and the reader will too.

6. **Create Dueling Motivations**—Give your villain and anti-hero similar motivations for doing what they do. Maybe both of them are trying to protect their family, even though they're on opposing sides. Who would be more right? This is conflict at its best.

7. **Stick Redemption Under Their Nose**—Give your villain or anti-hero a shot at redemption. What choice would they make?

8. **Give Them a Worthy Back-story**—Understand your villain's back-story. It's as important as your protagonist's. The reader must fully understand why they are motivated to do what they're doing.

9. **Make Them Vulnerable**—Pepper in a back-story that makes your anti-hero vulnerable—betrayed by love, lost an

important person in their life, or other tragic experience. Make them fearful of something, perhaps even themselves.

10. **Forge Them From Weakness**—Alcohol or drugs, adrenaline addict, insurmountable grief, or fear of the dark. Force them to battle with their deepest fears, making them worth someone's struggle to win them over.

11. **Make Them Corrupted by Life**—Have them see life through personal experiences that we can only imagine but they have lived through. Make trust an issue because they have been betrayed. They must be much more vulnerable than they are cynical to deserve the kind of significant other that it takes to open them up to someone else.

12. **Make Them Real**—To be real, they must have honest emotions. That means you, as an author, must delve into the murky corners of your own mind to get into their heads. It's not always an easy thing to do.

Getting to Know the Characters You Create

I've seen authors use a template of character facts and traits to set the facets of the main characters in their mind's eye. When I first started out, I found this practice helpful, although I did not find a good example of a template that worked for me in its entirety. So I'd say create one for yourself if you like this type of structure.

How does this work? I'm a visual learner, so creating these types of notes on my cast of characters can be useful to immerse myself into the world I will be creating. The subconscious brain retains much more than the conscious mind can recall. This process can set the foundation, allow you to absorb the details so your brain will run on autopilot once you begin to write. You can still learn or discover your characters as you go, but I found certain aspects of my characters become ingrained in my mind beforehand by using this questionnaire method.

The template might cover the facts of someone's life, such as:
- Where do they live?
- What work do they do? How much money do they make doing it?
- Who are their friends?
- Who are the people most influential in their lives?
- What habits do they have?
- What are their physical attributes?
- How do they dress?
- Where did they go to school—their educational level?
- What's in their wallet or purse?
- What type of car do they drive?

Although the above questions can be important, the most memorable characters come from the questions below.

Other questions that add depth to the characterization:
- What matters most to them?
- What would they die for?
- How do they deal with confrontation?
- What makes them vulnerable? What are their flaws and biases?
- What are their strengths?
- What's the one thing they would never do? (Of course, you'd make them do it in your plot.)
- What ethics do they have? Are they willing to bend them?

Another fun thing I do to reinforce characters in my mind is to create a photo board of images or the lifestyle/setting for my characters. This could be faces that I might get online or clothing or room settings. When I'm writing them, I have these images to look at. I may also be inspired by certain music. On the day I plan to write, I may listen to that music. Strange, but when you're channeling characters, anything goes.

When you are contemplating who your character will be, ask yourself what would set them apart from other characters in the genre you're writing. A clichéd two-dimensional character will never survive the crushing weight of an editor's slush pile. Become an observer in life and of people. Study what makes someone or something compelling then write the unforgettable story you've always wanted to tell.

Recommended Reading:
Goal, Motivation, & Conflict (GMC)—The Building Blocks of Good Fiction by author Debra Dixon (ISBN 0-9654371-0-8)—The book describes a matrix-type method to give your characters goals and motivation, and set up conflicts. It's a great resource to have when you're starting out and a good reminder for experienced authors too.

The Defining Scene—How to Introduce Your Main Character

I coined the phrase "defining scene" to describe a method I have used to introduce a main character in my books. This type of method is a technique used in the film industry. Picture Johnny Depp when he comes on the big screen for the first time in Pirates of the Caribbean. He doesn't merely walk on and deliver lines. He makes a splash and the moviegoer knows this character by how he makes his first appearance.

Make your main characters memorable. You only get one shot at a reader's first impression of your main characters. How do you set the stage?
- Devise a scene that gives your character a specific stage for them to perform—a showcase for them.
- Give them something to do that will show the reader who

they are.
- Encompass as much of your character in this scene—in one shot—so the reader knows exactly what makes them tick, their values, their likes and dislikes, and lays a foundation for the rest of the book.
- Focus on "character." This is not necessarily about "plot," unless you can devise a way that showcases your character and jumpstarts your plot, too.
- Build on the energy you've created with this introduction scene. If you put thought into this *Defining Scene*, the reader makes an investment in your character from that point forward.

The Defining Scene—Example

I created a character in one of my first manuscripts that was my take on an anti-heroine who is a modern Scarlett O'Hara. At the first part of the classic movie *Gone with the Wind*, Scarlett is self-centered and not very appealing as a central heroine. But of course, we all know how her journey ended. To this day, she endeared the name of Scarlett to people around the world.

My character, Justine, starts out with larceny on her mind while she's dining with an older man in a fancy restaurant. Working as an acquisitions and mergers specialist for a major corporation, she is first seen blackmailing a man to steal his energy company out from under him. She's ruthless and uses photos taken by a private investigator, shot while the man was with a young girl. To make matters worse, Justine has researched the man's prenuptial agreement and knows that if he is proven unfaithful, he'll lose everything. Needless to say, Justine is not a traditional heroine, but I infuse other aspects into the scene to manipulate the reader into liking her—or maybe not hating her as much—by the end of her "defining scene" introduction.

Below are key attributes and deliberate choices that I wrote into the scene to tip the scales in Justine's favor with the reader.

- She is opposite a very shady man who is worse than she is. He cheats on his wife and has affairs with under-aged girls. He's completely unscrupulous and even propositions Justine in the end. By comparison, she's an angel.

- Within the body of the scene, the reader learns more about Justine. She has a past I hint at. She is sensitive to the plight of the underage girl she accuses him of having an affair with. I save her past for later, but a hint is all the reader needs. Not much back-story is required. The hint teases the reader with a little mystery, too.

- Acting as a conspirator with Justine is a forthright young man, Graham, who is her assistant. The way I portray him is a really nice guy who cares and looks after his boss, despite her bad behavior. This manipulates the reader into seeing Justine the way Graham does. If Graham comes across as credible and sweet, these qualities pass to Justine by association.

- Because Justine kept Graham in the dark on what she had planned, she's seen as his protector too. She may be able to live with her "any means to an end" choices, but she doesn't force him to go along with her—for his sake.

- Justine comes off as vulnerable and sensitive, with an identifiable and self-deprecating humor readers can relate to. By the end of the scene, the things she values become more apparent. (I even considered having her take a doggie bag home for her pooch.)

- Justine may come across as a ruthless person at the start, but by the end of her defining scene, she is portrayed as a person who might champion a good cause, without a thought for money if it's for a valid reason.

I could have simply brought my female character into the story as a ruthless acquisitions employee, getting her assignment from her boss and wanting to dazzle him. Her boss is a man who wants to steal an inheritance out from under a nephew he's never met and is living off the grid in Alaska. Her boss lies to Justine about why he wants her to locate this guy. She would have gone off to Alaska in search of the missing heir, an urban goddess out of her element in the wilderness. That would have worked too, but I wanted the reader to wonder about her scruples. I also wanted her vulnerability to show from the start. I needed the reader to keep an open mind about who she is. Plus what happens at the beginning also comes back to bite her cute rear end as a plot twist. Everything comes full circle for a reason.

It takes thought to plot this type of scene, but remember it's the first scene for a major character. If you know your character, you will be able to construct a scene that will showcase their unique point of view in a memorable way.

Channeling Your Character—Free Association Method

This will sound strange, especially since this tidbit of advice is written into an author craft book, but bear with me. Honing your skills and being a sponge for ideas on writing is exciting, but don't let yourself become a perpetual student. The best way to learn about writing is by doing it.

I see many aspiring authors who write in fear that whatever they do won't be good enough. They believe published authors don't have the same doubts. *Baloney!* One of my favorite authors, Robert Crais, says that he constantly writes in fear, but he trusts the talent that got him to where he is. I have this written as an affirmation on my computer. We all have doubts. That's human nature, but if you're a storyteller, trust that talent and keep writing. Do it for yourself because that creative side of your nature matters.

But once you sit your butt down to write, don't over-think it. Don't be overwhelmed by rules or be burdened about whether or not you are doing things "the right way." That can strangle the life out of your story. Do the prep work on craft, but when it comes time to actually write it, take a flying leap off a cliff and let it all go. Allow your natural storyteller to be unleashed without filtering or censorship based on perceived rules or methods. Let your mind "channel" your story. I like to call it being "in the zone." I often will read back lines from scenes and not remember actually writing them. It feels like I'm channeling my characters. They tell me their stories and I'm merely their scribe.

I used to coach volleyball, for adults and kids. Practice sessions were conducted by running drills that would hone specific skill sets. The repetitive nature of those drills hopefully would become second nature to the team. Practices were designed to work on the skills needed, but once my team got on the court, I had to let them execute naturally. If they showed areas they needed to improve upon, I made a mental note to add that to our practices, but the game was not the time to chastise them for my failing them as a coach. It only showed me what to work on next practice. I was in it with them for the long haul and committed to improving their game and growing their confidence as self-assured athletes and people. I see writing in the same way. Do your prep work, but then go and play.

So how do you "channel" your character? I call this "free association." Imagine yourself in the head of your character as they come into a room, for example. Don't describe the room as if you were an outside observer taking inventory. Put your mind into the character and give them an opinion about what they are seeing. That's how our minds work, right? We don't come into a room and think, "A chaise lounge is to the right near a window, two chairs are in front of the desk..." Instead we might walk into that room and think, "Who the hell did the decorating in this dump? That ratty sofa's gotta be secondhand. The guy probably stole it out of a Goodwill bin." I call this "close third person" point of view—*and cynicism.*

A room is not just an inventory of the setting. Make it come alive with all the reader's senses from inside your character's head. Give your character an opinion. It will reflect the scene better and give insight into your character too. Make each word count and serve a multiple purpose to describe a more effective setting that adds voice and life to your prose.

Below is a before and after example:

Example—BEFORE—*Outside the Quonset hut, a generator kicked on and hummed. Inside, filth covered the windows and the acrid stench of cat piss filled Sam's nostrils. Cats dodged overturned tables and cardboard boxes. He followed McMurphy across the room, toward a rusty gas stove and a beat up metal desk with a cracked vinyl chair.*

Example—AFTER—*The annoying generator outside masked the sounds of the night, but once Sam got inside, the quiet of McMurphy's shithole closed in on him—and the stench. Ammonia from cat piss took his breath away and the little fur balls peered out of their dingy hiding places like vultures spying day old, hot off the asphalt, road kill.*

At the far end of the Quonset hut, a rusty gas stove kept company with a beat-up fridge and a cheap Formica table—each vying for the most useless award. Close by, file cabinets flanked a battered metal desk and shredded armchair. McMurphy never threw anything out. The man operated and lived in filth. A waste of skin like McMurphy would never make his Christmas card list.

Although the "before" description still works, the narrative reads like an inventory of the room and not from inside the character's head or Point of View (POV). It needs depth. By infusing your character and his opinions into the scene, you add distinctive color and voice. Plus, each word reflects not only the room, but the other character(s) as well and gives insight into your protagonist (the words serve a double and triple duty). Also, place the reader into the scene with all their senses by digging deep into your own personal experiences (what I call free association in your mind). Trust your gut and draft whatever comes to mind initially, like brainstorming. Let it flow, without censorship, and see what comes out. It works and it's fun!

Point of View—Wicked Good POV Can Get Your Freak On

Okay, I'll admit that when I first started writing, I had no idea what 'Point of View' (POV) was. I head hopped in a big way. I thought that's what writers did to show the reader what was in everyone's head, what they were thinking. I justified my lack of skill by saying that as long as a reader understood the story and didn't flip out with my POV gymnastics, that my poor technique would be acceptable. *Wrong!*

Years ago, after I read a blog post from an acquiring New York City editor (who was a believer in one character's POV per scene), I tried it and it completely opened my eyes to a new way to look at author craft. One POV per scene forced me to focus on one character and tell a mini-story within that scene, to move the plot or character insights forward. It can be a way of hiding plot twists or planting misdirection clues (red herrings) too. I tend to pick whose POV to write in by focusing on which character has the most to lose in that scene, but there are certainly other reasons to pick other characters too. Now, I've broken perceived "rules" plenty of times, for different reasons, but I think it's important to understand a method and try it to see how it can work for you before you simply dismiss it as "not your thing."

ONE AUTHOR'S AHA MOMENTS

I participate in a local critique group from time to time, mostly to stay connected to the writing community face-to-face. It's been fun. Great folks and eager writers. After hearing book chapters read aloud, I've come to the conclusion that aspiring authors should really master POV to enrich their storytelling and give a deeper look into the main characters. Understanding how POV can add depth and color to a character's voice can distinguish your work from countless others who submit to publishing houses every day. Every author makes decisions about POV in their books. If an author likes challenges, he or she may test their skill level and try different ways to convey a character's story as in the examples below.

THE BOOK THIEF by **Markus Zusak**, the book is about a 14 year old girl who lives during the time of the Holocaust and steals books to read. The narrator of the story is Death. As I've mentioned, this was one of my favorite young adult reads. The author took a risk to distance the reader from the 14 year old girl in the story. I thought it might have been a mistake when I started reading it, but with the gut wrenching subject matter, I later came to believe the reader needed that distance. And with Death as an outside observer, that brought a beautiful narrative voice (with a literary quality) to the story. In the end, I cried like a baby, despite the distance.

THIRTEEN REASONS WHY by **Jay Asher**, this story is about a girl who commits suicide, but leaves 13 audio tapes for the people who helped her make the decision to take her life. Great hook, right? The story is told through the eyes of one boy, but the structure is complicated by the ever present recorded voice of the dead girl, flashbacks to the past they shared, with jumps into the present while he spends one night without sleep, visiting all the places she put on a map. The intimacy of her voice often appears in one simple line or short spurts, mixed with the boy's POV. As a reader, I got sucked into this story and totally forgot I'm an author.

That's when I know the book is really good—and the author is amazing.

If Zusak and Asher had done the standard POV thing, their critically acclaimed books wouldn't be the same. I think it's important for authors to push the envelope on their craft, but it takes understanding the craft in order to know how to effectively "break the rules" with good results.

Okay, so here are my random thoughts on POV (from my POV):

1.) **The POV Tango Gets my Freak On**—Writing is a creative process and rigid rules don't always work, but after trying one POV per scene, I've learned when to utilize this technique and when NOT TO. In general, I'm a POV purest, but on the rare occasion that I shift POV in a scene, I usually transition it by an action where the reader's attention is diverted to the new player, such as with a handshake or a meaningful glare that shifts the focus over to the other character where the reader sees their reaction. Keep the break in POV simple by doing it the one time, not back and forth like a tennis match. I may also "break the POV rule" with one sentence, but I smile when I do that. Breaking the POV rule makes me feel frisky, but you can't fully appreciate a side trip down Freakalishess Boulevard unless you know what being "good" is, right?

2.) **Get into Heads like a Frontal Lobotomy**—Developing a full character "voice" is part of what I consider "deep POV." I've mentioned this before, but it bears repeating here. Average writers describe a setting as if they are detailing an inventory. Sure they touched on all the basics to trigger a reader's senses, but if they allow their minds to fully "free associate" the character's POV, the technique allows that character to have an opinion of his/her setting. That opinion adds color, depth to the scene, and reflects not only on his or her inner thoughts and nature, but it also sheds light on other characters too.

3.) **Crack the Whip, Dominatrix!**—Determining whose POV will dominate the scene can help direct your plot or give a different kind of insight into your main character. For example, red herrings (false clues) can be doled out through the POV of a character who doesn't know anything, or has a reason to lie. Or you can hide the guilt of someone by staying out of their "head." If you're stuck in one POV for the entire book—as in first person POV—you have limited options.

4.) **Boingee Boingee…*Whatever***—Head hopping bounces from character to character, removing the reader from building any great affinity or insight into any one character. This is reason enough to pick a POV per scene. Readers need to get emotionally involved and having a universal narrator describing the scene in omniscient fashion from afar can distance the reader from making any meaningful connection. This worked beautifully in *The Book Thief* as I mentioned, because the author told an emotionally charged story through an inventive character—Death—but for the average author, an omniscient POV can sever any hope of a reader connecting with your character(s).

5.) **Dogs are Better than People**—Picking the right POV can affect your research. If you don't feel comfortable writing a police procedural, establish the POV in a character at a crime scene who isn't a cop. They can be clueless for a reason and you can stay clear of research you don't feel is "your thing." Tell a dystopian, post-apocalyptic story from the POV of a dog. It could happen.

6.) Eenie Meenie Mynee Mo, Pick a Loser by the Toe—Selecting the right POV can shove the reader right into the middle of the action or put them in the backseat. For example, in a scene where a guy is undercover and on a stakeout, he could witness the abduction of a girl. An author could decide to stay in his POV or shift into the girl's head. Putting the reader into the victim's head could be scary and more emotional. You can always spring back into Mr. Action's POV and watch him come to her rescue, but I tend to pick POV by the character with the most to lose. In every scene, I make a choice for a reason. POV doesn't have to stay with the main character. Be open to new ways to tell a story.

7.) Name Your Poison—Combining first person with third person POV is tricky but can be done effectively if the transitions are clear. I first tried this in my YA debut book—*In the Arms of Stone Angels* (Harlequin Teen). I wanted to have the intimacy of a first person narrator through my central character, Brenna Nash, but I also wanted to bring my mystery/thriller techniques to YA and write third person POVs for other characters. The reason I chose to do this was to give the reader insight into some pretty nasty people, so the reader would fear more for my central boy and girl. I also wanted to hide clues to the mystery of who killed Heather. I combined first and third POV in another of my YAs, *On a Dark Wing* (Harlequin Teen), but after reading other YAs that mixed POVs, I added a tag to the start of every scene in first person. By doing this, I made the transitions easier for the reader to follow.

8.) Gender Two-Steppin'—In another of my next projects, I'm telling the story through TWO first person characters—a boy and girl. Each of their scenes will have their names at the start so the reader doesn't get lost. I wanted to be inside both heads to give a boy's and girl's perspective. The rest of the story will be told in third person, to allow me to hide clues and develop my plot. Confining a thriller author to one person's head (or even two) is unnatural.

Writing for a Series—Creating a Character and World to go the Distance

A strong trend in the publishing industry is the concept of a series—books that are linked through characters, plot, or world building—with a continuing story line. Many publishing houses read a concept or an author's voice and like it so much that they want to buy more than one book. Linking the books can also build readership or sustain an author's readers who are already familiar with their work.

So I thought it would be fun to examine ways to create a series character with enough creative juice to build or sustain a readership. Below are my thoughts:

- Paint a large enough canvass. Create a world that's big enough to allow a character to grow and surprise a reader with different plots scenarios.

- Give your main character(s) enough emotional baggage and personal conflicts that they can develop and grow from, to keep the series fresh.

- Make the plots in the series challenge your character's weaknesses or flaws. Conflict is vital for any book.

- Tie each plot to the character's emotional soft spots and allow the character to learn from what happens to them over the course of the series or be challenged by what happens, forcing them to deal with their flaws.

- Consider giving the main character one conflict or issue that continues through the series without resolution until the last book.

- Add a secondary cast of characters who add value. Make them fun, quirky, and definitely memorable, enough to bring a unique touch to your series. They are especially valuable if they add conflict or reflect on your main character's strengths or weaknesses. If your secondary characters are effective enough, this can mean spinoff potential.

- In any book, plant seeds for a spinoff story line. If the novel takes off, you can capitalize on your germinating ideas.

- Tell the reader enough in each book about the character's back-story to entice them to read your other books, but don't go overboard with a dump of information that will slow the pace. This can be a challenge to find the right blend of rehashing back-story to sticking with the new journey. Personally, I like to give the "feel" of key elements to the character's world with each book (as if it's standalone), but don't slow the pace by throwing everything back in.

- Avoid the formula. If something worked in book #1 in order to successfully launch your series, don't repeatedly recreate it. Surprise the reader with something new, which will keep your creative juices flowing too. Don't be so tied into your own success that you're afraid to surprise your readers.

- On the flip side, don't "jump the shark" that got you there. Surprising leaps in character motivation—just to add shock value without substance or believable motivation—

may stray too far from center to sustain your readership. Recognize your strengths and find new ways to hone them.

- Keep in mind that your character may have to age if the series becomes popular. Have a plan for that. Three books may wind up as twenty or more.

- Don't be afraid to dig deep inside yourself to fuel the motives or experiences of your character(s). Making them real is vital in order for a reader to connect with them, especially over a series.

- Don't wrap your character's journey up too neatly at the end of the series. Leave room for the reader's speculation on what the future may hold, so they can imagine his or her life moving on or picture what their love life might hold.

Chapter 4

Plot Structure—An Overview

It cracks me up that I'm even attempting to talk about plotting and structure. I am a "pantser" by nature, which means that I write on the fly "by the seat of my pants." When it comes to plotting out a book ahead of time in an outline form, I can't do it. I see books unfold in my head like a movie and I like to be surprised by the characters, their complicated motivations, and the layers of emotions that will be revealed as I write. But as a full time author, I've always kept my mind open to the idea of being organized before I begin actually writing a project.

After years of struggling to find something that works for me, I finally think I've hit on something that will work for "pantsers" like me. I also think people who enjoy plotting ahead of time can find merit in this method. It incorporates the 3-Act structure and storyboarding but doesn't have the extensive outlines I've heard about from other authors. I like the idea of committing to sticky notes that can be moved or thrown away. So below is my Author Bucket List on Plot Structure. I hope you like it, or modify it and email me through my website contact page on how it works for you. I'd love to hear from you.

To expose you to other ideas that I've looked at, I wanted to share some different key plotting structures I've worked with in my quest to get better organized. They are included in this chapter, along with a word of caution on formulaic methods for creating a book.

The Author's Bucket List on Plot Structure—For "Pantsers" and Plotters

As I've said, I've never been a plotter. I'm too impatient. Once I get the general idea of a story with a compelling conflict and a notion of my cast of players, I can't wait to "discover" the story as I write. It plays out in my head like a movie, but I'm constantly exploring new ways to get organized so my daily word count goals can be achieved without roadblocks.

In this book, I submit my latest (and ever-evolving) thoughts on plotting, involving the 3-Act Structure and the Storyboard method. These are purely my notions on combining these concepts as they can apply to my writing. Hopefully, you'll see elements you like in this for you.

I used to think of the 3-Act Structure as beginning, middle, and end, but I've read it more accurately reflected as Establish, Build, and Resolve by Michael Hauge in his book "*Writing Screenplays that Sell*." (I highly recommend Michael Hauge's books.) Thinking of these acts in this manner denotes movement. So imagine these three segments as buckets, but before I can toss wads of paper (or scenes) into these buckets, I must have a place to start.

Presuming I have a general notion of my book, I would create a list of 20-25 things I know about the action in my book in terms of what I call "big ticket" plot movements. No back-story. What will go on my list will be scenes that I envision as key elements to my story. They won't be put into any order. I merely list them as they occur to me. I would brainstorm without censoring my thoughts. I heard an author talk about creating notes on 3-M sticky notes, rather than a random list, but you get the idea. I don't expect to know every scene in my book at this stage. The storyboard I create will be an evolving beast that I will change as I write, edit, and finalize my book so I can see my plot at a glance.

Now let's talk about the 3-Act Structure in terms of a BIG "W."

ACT I—Establish—The start of Act I (or the top left of my "W") is the Triggering Event. It's the inciting incident that will start my story, the point at which my main character's life changes forever. As I travel down the left side of my "W," I head for the 1st Turning Point that usually sets up the problem or the first low point or perhaps a moment of hope. This is a reversal point that changes the direction of my plot as I head out of Act 1. In theory, I've "Established" my world up to this point and the general conflicts and players in the first 25% of my book.

ACT II—Build—As my plot heads toward the upward middle of my "W," that is another key reversal. If I have a book with hope in my first turning point, this shift might dash those hopes to some degree. If I have a dark moment in that first turning point, things get worse, but the plot takes another key turn one way or the other as the action "Builds." Act II ends with the next turning point (the 2nd low point of my "W"). This is the black moment where all seems lost. This part of the "W" represents the middle part of the turning point structure or 50% of my story, the "building" middle.

ACT III—Resolve—Now I would be in Act III, the last upward line of the "W" after the black moment. I'm headed toward "Resolution." In this section, my hero or heroine might discover something about the villain in the story that is their weakness. He or she might implement a plan to take advantage of this Achilles Heel, but I might consider throwing in another epiphany or twist before the end. This could be a twist or complication—an "Oh my, God" moment the reader might not see coming before the world is restored or the ending happens. This last part of the structure is the final 25%.

I've oversimplified these blended theories for the sake of this explanation. The lines of the "W" don't have to be linear, for example. I could have little ups and downs along the way that will take me through my book, but I wanted you to have a general idea of how this could work.

Now get ready with your buckets. Each of these acts is a bucket, for the purposes of this explanation. So each of the 20-25 brainstormed scenes I created at the beginning has a place in an Act Bucket. I would add to these 20-25 things as I get more familiar with my book, but if I were to Storyboard this out, I would create 20 squares that represent chapters in my books. (You might write differently, so make this work for you with your average number of chapters in a single-title book. Mine happens to be 20 chapters.) I would write my 25 items down with each one going on a 3-M Sticky Note and place them on my storyboard where I think they will go in Act I (25%), II (50%), or III (25%). Since each of these scene ideas is moveable, I can change the order and chapter they might appear to get the pace and build up the intensity. Once I see things on my storyboard in a visual manner, I will no doubt want to add more Sticky Note scenes to fill out the detail and transitions in my story as the plot develops.

I generally have 4-5 scenes in a chapter. So as my story plot movement gets established and builds toward a resolution, I can perhaps add colored notes to signify POV switches or character story arcs or relationship arcs to deepen my story understanding. This process can even fit with my "pantser" approach to structure with a simple method that I can see visually as I write and evolve the story. Writing software seemed too complicated to learn with my writing schedule, but I'd love to hear of a simple brainstorming plot method or storyboard concept if you have one.

9-Act Screenplay Structure—Plotting Resource

When I was looking for an interesting plot structure for fiction,

I found references to the 9-Act Screenplay Structure. This is the basic framework of today's blockbuster movies. You'll see 3-Acts and 12-Acts, but I played with the 9-Act version as a format and had some success in conceptually plotting one or two of my earlier stories. It's my belief that once your brain grasps the concept, you may automatically follow the idea whether or not you are aware of it. As a visual learner, it helped for me to draft this and embed it in my brain, like a time bomb triggered to go off when I sat in front of my computer.

The 9-Act structure is similar to the classic Hero's Journey that you may know about, but I thought this was an interesting approach for those who like structure.

9-Act Screenplay Structure

Act 0—During Opening Credits (First 5 Minutes of film)
   What strikes the conflict—sets it up—event years earlier may plant the seed of conflict

Act 1—Opening Image—The Panoramic Crane Shot (Next 5 Minutes)

Act 2—Something Bad Happens (5 Minutes)
   In a crime story, it's usually the murder—reveal the bad front man, but hold off on the introduction of the bad head honcho until later

Act 3—Meet Hero/Protagonist (15 minutes)
   Meet hero—give him 3 plot nudges to push him to commit

Act 4—Commitment (5-10 Minutes)
   The push—Usually one scene that's a door to Act 5—one-way door, no turning back

ONE AUTHOR'S AHA MOMENTS

Act 5—Go for wrong goal (Approx. 30 minutes)
> A series of 8-12 min. cycles called "bams" or complications followed by a rest period of 5 minutes or so to uncover some of the back-story. End this act with the lowest point for the protagonist. The dark moment.

Act 6—Reversal (5-10 Minutes—Usually 70 Minutes into the Film)
> The last clue discovered—Now Act 2 makes sense—It is the low point, a history lesson usually revealed by the bad guy/honcho—but reveals the Achilles heel of the nemesis too.

Act 7—Go for New Goal (15-20 Minutes)
> The clock is ticking—hero has a new plan. The action seesaws back and forth with nemesis and hero gaining and losing ground between each other—usually takes place in 24 hours within the context of the movie. Favors are repaid, magic, good luck happens. The new plan is kept secret. New goal is achieved.

Act 8—Wrap it Up (5 minutes)
> Back to where it all began—a feeling of accomplishment and rebirth—the world restored. Ahh!

Word of Caution: Pitfalls of Using a Formula

Now having outlined this plotting structure, I'm not sure if following something like this (without deviation) would hamper creativity by providing too much framework. This would be like "the rules" of writing. Maybe rules are there to be understood, but we shouldn't be afraid to break them either. Keep your mind open to new ideas or twists into your plot. Be daring.

Recommended Reading

"Writing Screenplays that Sell" by Michael Hauge—ISBN: 0-06-272500-9

"Screenwriting Tricks for Authors (and Screenwriters)" by Alexandra Sokoloff—ASIN: B0032JSJ9U

Also follow Alexandra Sokoloff's blog "The Dark Salon" that highlights screenwriting tips for authors—http://thedarksalon.blogspot.com/

Chapter 5

Pacing Your Novel

The concepts I will share with you now on writing a thriller and the seduction of mystery can be used to create a page-turning book for any genre. These are epiphanies I had while writing or reading about the craft of writing. I try to incorporate new things in each project to keep writing a challenge and a learning experience for me. Even though I may share thriller craft with you, think of how these tips can work in other genres.

Create a Page Turner in Any Genre – Four Tips

I thought it would be important to share the basic structure of how words appear on the page and how chapters and scenes play a part in making your book "feel" like a page turner. As a reader, you might not notice the following tips, but as an author, you should think about incorporating these elements into your story.

> **1.) Shorter Chapters**
> When I first started writing, my chapter lengths were approximately 6,500 words. As I wrote more suspense, my chapters became tighter and my average word count lowered to 4,500 words. Some authors use only a scene per chapter. That's not something I like to do. I tend to use shifting scenes to create a sense of urgency during action sequences or to give an illusion of pace, so I don't do the

one scene chapter, but shortening chapters can certainly add to the feeling of pace.

Another reason to have shorter chapters is based on how people read books. (I read like this, so I can speak from personal experience.) Nights are when I enjoy reading the most. Books are part of my bedtime ritual and it relaxes me, even when I'm reading about serial killers or zombies. Committing to read a short chapter is easy. Readers look ahead to see if the next chapter is short. If it is, they sometimes read on. That's how readers end up finishing a book at 1:00 AM. That's when they send you an email that you kept them up AGAIN. (I sincerely apologize for destroying their sleep, but I'm never really *that* sorry.) Short chapters serve many purposes.

2.) White Space—Shorter Paragraphs and Dialogue

A reader's eye tends to seek out dialogue if an author's narratives are too long. I believe in creating white space on the page so a reader doesn't get bogged down with weighty paragraphs. It makes the page seem simpler to read for people who might want to read "just a little more." White spaces, shorter paragraphs, and sharp concise dialogue all work together so the reader feels they can read on.

3.) Split Scenes and Anticipation

This is a favorite technique of mine. Whether you write suspense books or not, the idea of splitting the action of a scene, in a compelling way, forces the reader to make a decision on whether they keep reading. Make it impossible for them to put your book down. This can be a true cliffhanger moment where the character might be in great peril, or it can be simply a moment where a mystery will be revealed. Don't rush it. Less is way more.

The idea of "reader anticipation" can be applied to a Young Adult novel if the author writes a scene at the end of a chapter where a mysterious boy is about to be revealed to the young heroine, for example. Savor that moment and split the scene into the top of the next chapter so the reader feverishly must turn the page to see what happens. Or add mystery by being patient in revealing an element of the truth to keep the reader eagerly anticipating what happens next. Any genre can benefit by this pace method.

4.) Chapters and Scenes as Mini-Stories
I believe that an author should place as much importance on the start of each chapter and each scene as they do the first line of a book. Typically, an author sweats over that key first line in their novel. It can definitely be important, but why waste an opportunity to make an impression on the first lines of chapters or scenes? Chapters and scenes are like mini-stories. They have a beginning, middle, and an end. The reader is taken on a journey through those shorter segments that moves them forward into your plot. If you treat the start of any chapter with the same quality as you would the beginning of your book, the reader will also get a greater experience and not want to put your book down.

Thriller Authors Aren't Normal!—Ten Writing Tips that Can Make You One of Us

I'm here to confess that as a thriller author I'm not a well person. Bad men speak to me in my head—and I like it. I scare myself all the time. It's my job. Who says crime doesn't pay? And I openly admit that I torture fabricated people with my computer keyboard. In short, what lands most people behind prison bars can put me on a fictional happy train.

That's because thriller authors don't think like normal people. We have a warped sense of reality and of what's funny. I play deviant games of "what if" scenarios in my head, like what if the Internet could melt your brain and make it seep out of your ears? Or what if coffee shops dispensed mind-altering lattes or espresso was discovered as the sole source of global warming? In the world of fiction, these things can happen. But once you get the great idea for a novel, what's next? How can you pull it all together enough to interest a publisher?

For aspiring authors everywhere, I've put together TEN TIPS that I hope you'll find useful in crafting your book. Add a little pace and structure to your brilliant plot and you may join the ranks of published thriller authors who are borderline psychotics, like me. Everyone has got to have goals.

1—**Start with a BANG!**
Start your book with the moment that changes the character's life forever or throw the reader into the middle of action, using all their senses. Shorter sentences will also add tension when your character is holding a ticking time bomb, but stick with the action and be patient with dropping mystery clues. For suspense, action sequences are not the time to introduce back-story or a lot of description. You'll have time to explain later. If your character is ducking gunfire, avoid telling the reader about his misspent youth or describing the posh setting that he's about to bleed over.

2—**Something Bad is Coming**
Filmmaker Alfred Hitchcock pioneered many film techniques in suspense and psychological thriller genres. He believed suspense didn't have much to do with fear, but was more the anticipation of something bad about to happen. When I read this, it was a huge epiphany for me. The idea changed how I thought about scene and chapter endings. (Remember the movie scene where the woman is about to open the door and everyone in the theatre screams,

"*DON'T OPEN THE DOOR!*" Of course, she always does, but once the door is opened, everything is known.) Don't give the reader a chance to put down your novel at the end of a chapter. Hook them into turning the page. Give them a sense of foreshadowing or plant the seed of a red herring to sustain the pace and tease them with things to come.

3—Enter Late, Leave Early

Enter Late, Leave Early (ELLE) is a concept that maintains pace and transition in the scene of a book and leaves the reader wanting more. ENTER LATE refers to starting a scene in the middle of the action, such as a cop already at the murder scene staring down at the body, not a scene that shows him or her driving over to the crime. LEAVE EARLY refers to a scene ending that foreshadows something or raises a question or creates more of a mystery, not showing the detectives driving back to the police station. Quick snippets of plot suggest pace and movement. The reader's mind will fill in the gaps on what happened in between. If you've ever read a good screenplay, you will see how readily your mind fills in the gaps of setting, action, and the emotional elements of a character through the predominant use of dialogue. (Note: This ELLE principle does not apply to dialogue. Don't make the reader guess what your characters are talking about. Begin at a logical starting point to the conversation for clarity.)

4—Torture your Characters

Yes, you read this right. Torture your characters. It's legal and fun. Make the reader understand why you chose your character to be the star of your novel. In suspense, they have to rise to the occasion—even if they are an average Joe or Josephine—and go up against insurmountable odds.

5—No One Likes a Cheater

Don't rely on surprise suspects or miraculous databases to add twists to your plot. That's cheating. We all laugh when a TV crime show or movie can process DNA analysis in seconds or the crime scene technicians have access to amazing databases that don't exist. Or in fantasy, when a character suddenly develops a magical power when they need it, even though they never showed the ability before. *How convenient!* Such inventive technology allows the TV detectives to wrap up the TV show in minutes—or in that fantasy example, a character can be saved more by author intrusion and coincidence than by any true ability—but that's not how it should work. Don't get lazy with your research and don't resort to this kind of "cheating." There are no short cuts to a solid plot with well-motivated characters.

6—Pile it on, Baby!

Conflicts add drama. Put up roadblocks and heap on the complications by capitalizing on the internal and external conflicts for your character. Force a guy afraid of heights to scale a tower to save a child. Or compel a shy, timid woman to pick up an AK-47 and shoot her way out to rescue her family. Give your characters baggage the reader can relate to. Force your character out of their comfort zone with emotional obstacles that enable them to do amazing things and become a real star in your book. (Remember that torture is good in fiction. Say it aloud until you believe it, "Torture is good." It's liberating.) Action by itself can be boring if you don't add the right balance of human struggle and compelling emotion into a story.

7—Escalate the Stakes and Make it Personal

In good suspense, the stakes intensify. As an author, you want your reader to feel a physical excited reaction when they read your book. To do this, it helps to put a face on the victim. In my book, *Evil Without a Face*, a 17-year-old girl is lured from home by an online predator pretending to be another young girl. You've heard this story before, but I catapult a troubled Alaskan family into a massive global conspiracy with the clock ticking. A tangle of unlikely heroes attacks this conspiracy from different angles and they converge in a fight for their lives. The conspiracy is far-reaching, it's deadly, and because one young girl is caught up in a web of lies, it's personal.

8—Tick Tock Goes the Clock

Give your characters a deadline—a race against time—then shorten the timetable. The story is even more compelling when you force your character to make really tough decisions. Make them do the one thing they would *NEVER* do with an unthinkable consequence looming as the clock is ticking.

9—Everyone Loves a Big Finish

If you build up the hype on your book, give the reader a big finish. Don't disappoint them with an ending that doesn't live up to expectations. Also tie up the loose ends for reader satisfaction. I'm not only referring to the clues being resolved, but the emotional journey should be tied up too.

10—Restore the world? That's up to YOU

Redemption at the end of a book can be good as well as uplifting. I like the idea of restoring the world that an author creates, but it doesn't always have to be the same world. Crime affects people in a bad way and it radiates out like ripples on still water with many people affected—from the victim to the family survivors to cops investigating the case. Don't be afraid to show the aftermath.

I know by now you're thinking that I really love what I do. For the sake of my mental health, I'm conflicted, I suppose. Weighing the strange consequences of being a thriller author has not been easy, but I'm optimistic that I can strike a balance and retain the sanity I have left—or be forced to find a whole new set of friends.

The Seduction of Mystery—Make It Work For You

No matter what genre, a book can always seduce a reader with the titillation of mystery. Elements of mystery can be woven into a YA by presenting a main character with an unexplained back-story that is revealed slowly into the book or the series. A suspense or thriller plot can race towards the end with its escalating stakes, but the lure of an underlying mystery teases the reader and holds them tight as the storyline unfolds to reveal its fleshy curves and tantalizing secrets. The seduction is made more complete and satisfying.

In a seduction, back-story is the equivalent of smoking a cigarette after everything is over. An author needs to titillate with the lure of mystery for as long as possible. Like foreplay and flirtation, this is the notion of "reader anticipation" and it changed how I thought about scenes and chapter endings. At some point, you want the reader to know everything and have a satisfying experience, but it's "anticipation" that drives you to turn those pages all night long. There's no faking that.

If you're a writer, anticipation doesn't have to only be about big plot movements. Don't forget the voyeur in all of us, readers and writers alike. Relationships need a story arc too. Conflict and tension make them more delectable. Our main characters are tested, tortured, pushed to the limits. When a man and woman are involved in a personal relationship, a writer makes them pay for wanting to be together.

On my upcoming YA project—*Indigo Awakening* (Harlequin Teen)—I had a choice to make. I could have unfolded the story by relying on the suspense plot to be the main driver—or I could present my characters by their actions, without explaining the reason for their behavior until I absolutely had to. I chose to make my characters' back stories a strong mystery component where the plot will eventually force them into revealing themselves to each other and the reader. I'm orchestrating a seduction, one garment at a time. With some elements for key secondary characters, I layer the mystery without even knowing the answers myself. What an incredible rush! I can't wait to see what happens.

Scene Structure for Pacing—Building an Onion from the Inside Out

Ever thought about building an onion from the inside out? (Come on. Humor me.) That's a visual for a method I use to frame out a scene with dialogue. For a scene where dialogue is key, I like to focus on it completely, so I developed a way to do that. The exercise of writing the dialogue first came from having to split my time between my day job and writing. On my special writing days, I'd grab lunch by myself and take a notepad with me. (I wasn't really alone. Like Sybil, writers never are.)

People would always comment that my scenes jumped right into the action with sharp concise dialogue. In trying to explain to another writer how I did this, I had to understand it myself. That's when I understood how much my little lunchtime exercise had trained my brain to think this way.

I had broken apart the dialogue from the rest of the narrative to work on it separately as a more efficient use of my time before I got home that night to finish the scene. Consequently, the dialogue got my full attention and I usually tended to visualize the scene in my head as a TV program or movie.

1. **FIRST**—Use dialogue as the framework for the scene
   - Consider writing the dialogue first so you can concentrate on it (Use this as an exercise only. Once you get this down, you won't need to do this time and time again.)

   - Make the dialogue important. There is nothing like witty banter or a clever verbal skirmish between two adversaries. Avoid chit chat or back-story dumps disguised as dialogue. You won't be fooling the reader.

   - If your character confronts someone at a high school reunion that they haven't seen in twenty years when they buried a body after prom, you better have them say more than, "Gee, nice sweater." Chitchat would never happen in real life, given this situation, unless these two people are guiltless serial killers. (That actually sounds like a fun idea. Serial killers at a reunion.) Too much introspection can kill the impact of their first meeting. Personally, I like a challenge like this and don't get me started on the whimsical world of the serial killer. But think about it—what *WOULD* they say to each other?

2. **SECOND**—Body Language/Action
   - Body language can be fun, especially if it contradicts what the character is saying in dialogue—Use it! Manipulate it!

   - Be concise and not too wordy with action, but keep it real. If guns are blasting, remember your characters are dodging bullets, not engaging in witty banter. *Bullets stop for no man...or woman!!!*

3. **THIRD**—Mood and Setting—Use it to accentuate what's happening.
    - I love the mood created with a great setting. It can embellish the emotion in a scene or add an underlying tension (i.e., an escalating storm or a well-placed gust of wind against a silk blouse or skirt). The beauty is in the details.

4. **LAST**—Emotional layering—Introspection
    - Give your character a journey through the scene. Don't just repeat the same old thoughts over and over in different ways, no matter how clever you are. Have their introspection grow or change.

    - Too much introspection, for me as a reader, slows the pace. But if an editor wants it, read my first point over again and build upon the emotional layers with new material. Insights into a character can be a wonderful gift to your reader.

5. **THEN STAND BACK AND TAKE A LOOK—What is there? Do you have a whole ONION or a lemon?**
    - Make every scene into a tight mini-story with a hook beginning, elements that propel the plot forward, and a memorable page-turning end. Or end it with a beautiful image a reader will remember and feel long after they've put the book down.

    - Or stop in the middle of the action and continue it on the top of the next chapter.

    - You are in control of your story's layout. Make it interesting.

Chapter 6

Does Your Book Have a Hook?

I've heard the term "hook" used in many ways from developing your initial book inspiration (the most intriguing aspect of your book) to creating an "elevator pitch" for agents in a quick one-line way that might intrigue them to ask to see more of your work. In my opinion, the most important aspect of a hook is in how you come up with your book. If you have a real hook crafted into your novel, the elevator pitch and query letter summary will come. So let's focus on that.

What is a Hook?

To define a hook, I thought I would list some YA books and give examples of very effective hooks. I'm an avid reader of YA and would still be, even if I didn't write it. The YA books today are well-written and the edgy subject matter appeals to me.

1. ***THE HUNGER GAMES, CATCHING FIRE, MOCKINGJAY*** by Suzanne Collins—A futuristic tale told through the eyes of a young girl in a post-apocalyptic world where the government demands two sacrificial tributes (gladiators, one of each sex) from each of its territories, for a televised reality show fight to the death.
   The Hook—Teens fighting to the death in a Post Apocalyptic televised reality TV show. The post-apocalyptic time period

is very popular in YA, but what struck me with this series description is "teens fighting to the death on a reality TV show." I had to know more and it shocked me. You know there will be graphic violence, but telling the story through the eyes of one girl makes this series gut-wrenching. Kids shouldn't have to fight to the death. It made me wonder what kind of world would allow that to happen.

2. **THE MATCHED *trilogy*** by Ally Condie—In this trilogy a young girl is faced with a society that makes decisions for her and how she will live. The burden of choice is taken away from her. It's not until she discovers that her Matched microchip produces a different boy's face as her ideal match that she begins to question everything.
The Hook—A futuristic society plays God in determining a person's fate. What happens when your freedom is taken away? How far would you go to get it back, even when your family, friends, and society is against you? This David versus Goliath theme is intriguing.

3. ***IF I STAY*** by Gayle Forman—After a tragic car accident, a young girl loses her entire family and is in a coma in the hospital, but she's aware of everything that is happening and must find the will to stay with the living or let go and die .
The Hook—A girl in a coma must make a choice to live or die after she loses everything. This book is smartly written with intelligent characters, but doesn't that hook make you want to read how she makes her decision and why?

4. **THE HOUSE *of* NIGHT *Vampyre Series*** by P. C. Cast and Kristin Cast—The series chronicles the life of fledgling vampyre Zoey Redbird as a young Cherokee girl attends a very special school to learn what becoming a vampyre will mean.

The Hook—Vampyre finishing school. If you don't graduate from this school, you die. Enough said. P. C. Cast is a former high school teacher. I think she had fun with this premise. When this series started, it was very unique as far as the Vampyre school goes. Others have since copied that premise, but the series remains unique for its incorporation of Cherokee myths and legends into the story line.

How to Define Your Hook

You can write the book first and determine your hook afterwards, but I think it's most important to understand the concept of hook and develop one for your novel before you begin writing it. If your hook is unique enough, it will set your hair on fire with the need to write it. *True inspiration!* A hook can come from unique settings, special characters, compelling time periods, or gripping conflicts.

Below are questions that might help you in determining your hook:
1. What will be unique about your book?
2. What is your main conflict?
3. How is your time period unique?
4. What is the main emotional thread in your novel?
5. What will set your story apart from others in your chosen genre?
6. Who are the main characters? List 3-5 adjectives that would describe them.
7. Will your story narrator be unique?
8. Will your lead character be forced into making a compelling choice?
9. How will your world building be different?
10. Will your characters or world be filled with either unique powers or "rules" to live by?

If you are determining the answers to these questions prior to writing your book, these questions should take you time to develop. A well-crafted hook can get you noticed in a slush pile of queries/proposals that an agent or editor slogs through every day. Take your time with this before you start writing and you'll have an advantage later when it's proposal time.

Creating a Logline

The term "logline" comes from the entertainment industry and is used in written form as TV program listings or in the film industry as "pitch" lines that a screenplay writer might use to hook a studio exec into financially supporting a proposed movie idea. In a one to two sentence logline, the concept could be something as simple as "Demon killer Van Helsing gets sucked down the rabbit hole into Alice in Wonderland" or "Sex in the City meets Thelma and Louise on a road trip." If the movie references are well-known, this kind of description could vaguely click with an editor or agent, but I think this type of description needs something more added to solidify it.

I use a logline concept in starting a synopsis. It provides an overview of the project in a succinct fashion that can be used in other ways as I mention below. Here are examples of some of my short book descriptions where adjectives are used to describe a protagonist. Character names aren't generally used in a logline unless the character is known to the reader or is a continuing character in a series.

> **No One Heard Her Scream**—A relentless detective barred from the investigation into the abduction and murder of her sister is forced to take another case. But when she finds skeletal remains buried in the wall of an old theatre are from a woman close to her sister's age, the hunt for a killer becomes a vendetta for justice.
>
> **No One Lives Forever**—A mysterious woman assassin barges into a man's Chicago flat, attempting to collect an old marker, begging his help to free a man kidnapped in Brazil. He's got seven days to attempt an impossible rescue of the father he never knew.

Evil Without A Face—Two unlikely heroes join forces to save a seventeen-year-old girl from an insidious global conspiracy—a faceless new kind of evil.

It's not easy paring down your whole book into a 1-2 line description, but give it a try. Make every word count and delete anything that can be left out to make it sparse yet descriptive. These short descriptions can be used on your website, in query letters, or as book jacket summaries, as I show in the examples below:

The Echo of Violence *(Sweet Justice Series Book #3)*— Terrorists attack a Haitian missionary school fundraiser to take hostages, forcing Sentinels' agent Alexa Marlowe into an unlikely alliance with a relentless mercenary.

In the final book jacket summary for The Echo of Violence, you can see how the logline description got incorporated into the book summary printed on the cover.

The man she'd trust with her heart could sabotage everything...

When terrorists attack a Haitian missionary school, brutally killing their hostages and posting videos of the senseless murders online, time is running out. Sentinels' agent Alexa Marlowe is forced into an unlikely alliance with a relentless mercenary. But he is no stranger.

Jackson Kinkaid witnessed the raid, and only he can track the killers to their mountain stronghold. Guarding a dark secret, rumored to sell his services to the highest bidder, Jackson is not the same man Alexa once knew. And although he can lead her to the terrorist leader she's been ordered to take alive, how can she be sure he won't sabotage

ONE AUTHOR'S AHA MOMENTS

her mission to save the one person who got him through the worst nightmare of his life?

In the short description of an upcoming series (The Hunted) I have with Harlequin Teen slated for 2012-2013, you can see how a logline helped frame the book jacket summary. That summary is below. The top bold line—*"Because of what you are, the Believers will hunt you down"*—is a dialogue quote from the YA book that highlights the main conflict in the story. You can also see the tagline the publisher will use on the front cover and in other promotion. The tagline is—*They are our future—if they survive...*

Indigo Awakening (Book #1—*The Hunted Series with Harlequin Teen*)— When Lucas Darby becomes the prime target of a fanatical church that hunts psychic Indigo kids, his sister Rayne finds her only ally is a mysterious runaway boy with unimaginable powers that could doom them all.

Because of what you are, the Believers will hunt you down.

Voices told Lucas Darby to run. Voices no one else can hear. He's warned his sister not to look for him, but Rayne refuses to let her troubled brother vanish on the streets of LA. In her desperate search, she meets Gabriel Stewart, a runaway with mysterious powers and far too many secrets. Rayne can't explain her crazy need to trust the strange yet compelling boy—to touch him—to protect him even though he scares her.

A fanatical church secretly hunts psychic kids—gifted "Indigo" teens feared to be the next evolution of mankind—for reasons only "the Believers" know. Now Rayne's only hope is Gabe, who is haunted by an awakening power—a force darker than either of them imagine—that could doom them all.

They are our future—if they survive...

Chapter 7

The Writer's Life

The Writer's Life, Goal Setting, and Editing
I wanted to leave you with my parting thoughts on the writer's life. I write every day. Even when I'm relaxing between projects, my writer's mind is always thinking of plots, characters, atmospheric settings, or dialogue because I love doing it. I've become more of a listener and an observer, which has elevated the quality of my life. Writing has become an unexpected passion, so I make time for it.

I'm a procrastinator by nature. Always have been, but I've found that by setting daily attainable writing goals by word count, that I can make progress and feel good about it. If I don't hit the mark one day, I make up for it the next or I adjust my forward daily goals to make sure I meet my contractual deadline. Writing is hard enough to do without beating myself up over goals that shouldn't be a punishment. While I'm writing a book, I set up a spreadsheet of daily word count goals so I can see my progress. I aim for a total of 90,000 words per novel (since I write single-title books) and whittle down what remains with a solid word count each day.

Some authors believe in editing a book in drafts. This means they write fast and get the basic plot on the page, from start to end. Then they edit from start to finish in draft stages until they are satisfied.

I can't work that way. I edit as I write. I may edit a scene dozens of times but when I do it a little each day, I can eventually move on. I don't stop my forward writing. Writing forward is always my daily goal, but I may edit the 1-2 prior chapters until I am satisfied with them, and move forward with my edits. You might think of this as a rolling edit process.

After I write a chapter, my first pass is usually to delete. I edit and tighten my wording before I layer in deeper emotion, add more succinct character motivation, or clarify plot points that drive each scene forward. If I discover a cool twist later in the book that I'd like to build into earlier parts of the book, I "thread" them in to give the reader hints or clues so I don't hit them cold with the twist. Editing thoroughly as I go, in a rolling fashion, allows me to see these things more clearly. For me to work in drafts, it feels as if I'm leaving mistakes on the page and I can't stand that. I want my "rolling edits" to make a difference so that when I am getting towards the end of my book I know I am done. I don't want to revise draft after draft or have to delete large sections because of later edits. When I've finished a book, I want to move on to the next project.

Do You Believe in Writer's Block?
I refuse to acknowledge writer's block. It's too easy to blame an affliction we seemingly have no control over. I prefer to think my brain is secretly trying to tell me something that I'm not hearing, even though we are close neighbors.

When I can't hear my brain SCREAMING at me to stop writing—apparently my body can hear that pesky three pounds of mush—my fingers boycott me. They quit hitting the keyboard or I find many excuses to distract myself—even doing laundry, for crying out loud. Now that's desperate.

I've learned to listen to my body when this happens. It's my interpreter when it comes to "brain speak." One way to get me back on track is first to understand and accept that my brain is niggling me about the plot, character revelation/motivation, or certain scenes aren't working and could be better. Usually this part only lasts hours or a day or two, or a good night's sleep. I've found answers for my dilemma in commercials, the NOVA channel, and I even found the complete ending for a book from watching an old skateboard flick, starring Christian Slater, called "Gleaming the Cube."

But when I can't find the answer alone, I've found a tried and true method is cornering anyone to listen to me explain it to them. Usually this poor person is my husband. We can chat over breakfast, spending quality time talking about how to kill people and get away with it, or he listens to my ramblings as we drive. (Your gas mileage may vary.) One thing amazes me about this process. It doesn't seem to matter who I corner or how I explain it, I invariably come up with the answer on my own as I talk it out. It seems the brain needs the mouth to communicate back to my brain. What a weird Détente!

If you haven't tried this, do it. It will blow your mind. Literally! I've concluded that since I spend most of my day in my own head—without speaking—that when I finally *do* speak, my brain is listening. It finally sends messages that result in solutions. Things I wouldn't have explored purely thinking about them. Apparently explaining things to someone outside my "brain trust"—whether the person ultimately contributes to the process or not is irrelevant—it forces me to work things out in a way I can't do on my own. The act of being more thorough in my explanation seems to be a critical element to my process.

But given the old adage about a tree in the forest, does it take someone else listening to get results to my dilemma? Or is this the first stages of schizophrenia and my way of justifying it? I haven't ranted to me, myself, and I on this yet. That day might come on its own—along with a nice helping of meds.

A Word to Teens Who Write

Every time I meet a young author who wants to write a YA novel, I am in awe. I wish that I had been *that* driven when I was a teen, but the YA fiction market did not exist as it does today. Reading these great offerings now must be an amazing inspiration to young writers. I know these books are to me.

If you're an avid reader, you might consider starting a blog where you review books that you read. This would allow you to combine your love of reading with writing a review that breaks down what you liked about the book or what didn't work for you. Blogs are free and many publishers offer free books to online reviewers with impressive blogs. This could be a win/win/win for you, the publisher, and the authors you admire.

As for your writing, my advice is to keep writing, no matter what form you do that in. If you write in a journal or do short stories or poetry, I would advise that you stay plugged into your creative brain. Record your thoughts on feelings, people, places you've been, with an eye on describing them as you would as an author. All of this will form a foundation for the voice you will have as a writer.

Teachers will give you creative writing homework assignments or essays. You may not always see the point or like the assignment, but do them all and do them well. You can always stay true to the voice you are building on your own through your journal writing or short stories or novels. Find a way to express yourself by writing the kinds of books you want to read and keep working at it. It's like exercising a muscle.

The Reality of Book Promotion

I'm bringing up book promotion in this author craft book to emphasize the importance of having a business sense when it comes to promoting your books. Whether you self-publish or have a traditional publisher buy your book, you still will need a realistic view for getting the word out.

With each book release, I try new ways to promote my novel. I ditch what doesn't work and I'm constantly looking for cost effective ways to reach the largest number of readers. For my debut young adult release, for example, I had a marketing strategy to launch my debut YA that encompassed four pages of a varied promo effort directed at indie stores, libraries, professional organizations, online social media, my mailing list, etc.

Book promotion has changed over the years and the developments are coming even faster as we trend up in the digital world. I have an e-reader now too, which has drastically changed how I buy books and how I hear about novels that interest me. So how does the average author today promote their own book in this evolving business?

This usually translates to online promotion since it's free (except for the time you put into it). Focusing your marketing and branding efforts online can be an effective means to get the word out to the right people. On my recent summer reading tour with fellow Texas YA authors, we had a tour blog set up a couple of months prior to our events that garnered thousands of hits and counting. A book signing might have ad promo and get people to come see you, but the exposure is greater online where website traffic can be hundreds or thousands of hits a day with the post continuing to get hits even after the book signing is over. And with a reader already online, they can click on a link and buy your book, or download a sample to their e-reader that might entice them to buy the rest of your novel. This doesn't mean the book signing is dead. It just means

ONE AUTHOR'S AHA MOMENTS

authors have choices on how they spend their time.

Online Marketing I've Found Effective:
1. **A professional looking website or blog**—Blogs are free if money is tight and you can share the work by putting together a group blog of authors who write similar genres.

2. **Twitter**—Get to know your regional review bloggers. They can be great support. If you tweet teasers for your blog posts or news on your books or giveaways, you can actually track hits off twitter feeds when twitterville goes to your blog or website and gauge your effectiveness with "stats" from a stat counter embedded in your website or through your blog stats.

3. **Facebook**—I dislike Facebook (FB). There, I said it. Facebook has Fan Pages for authors, but the way FB changes the rules without notice, has privacy issues, and inhibits how you conduct business on their system with non-user-friendly quirks, I don't use it. I find there are better ways to spend my time.

4. **Other Social Media**—There are other ways to get your name out there, like Tumblr, Google+, Linked-In, Pinterest, etc. I have used some of these, but I don't spend time at it. These outlets require maintenance and updating. I tend to use methods for which I can track the usefulness. As a writer, it's far more important for me to write. Novel concept, right (pun very much intended)?

5. **Goodreads**—If you don't have an author page here, why not? It's free and you can link your blog to your Goodreads author page to keep material fresh without much effort. Any member here is a reader. You can also run contests on Goodreads, but you must follow their rules.

6. **Amazon Author Central**—Did you know that you can update your own Amazon author/book page for reviews, book endorsement blurbs, etc.? You don't have to wait for your publisher to do it.

7. **Rafflecopter**—This is a very cool promotional tool that I have grown to love. (Here is the link: http://www.rafflecopter.com/). Bloggers use it to run contest giveaways. Make contact with Rafflecopter and request to become a member. It takes time to hear back, but it's worth it. In the Rafflecopter form, you can set up mandatory and optional ways for participants to enter your contest, such as "follow me on twitter or my blog," and/or "tweet about entering my contest" to stir buzz. Include links for them or draft their tweet format to make it easy and the contest will run itself. Also spell out the rules, such as whether the giveaway is open to international entrants (added shipping costs) or domestic only, or what dates the contest will run. Once your contest ends, you can use Rafflecopter to randomly pick a winner through *Random.org* and the form will also announce winners. With more and more people using this form, it makes contests easy and more effective for authors.

The simple truth is that most authors won't see a great deal of promotion dollars from their publisher. You'd think that if a house were taking on a new author and book that they would include a certain amount of money geared for promotion, but the reality is that the publisher spends generic dollars on promoting their line of books or other authors' works and hopes readers will notice your book in the process. They rely on the author doing their own promotion. It's quite conceivable that the average author will spend more to promote their book than their publisher will, especially given that houses are tightening up on advances.

So as authors look seriously at self-publishing and e-books, it's tempting to cut back on all the time consuming and resource-depleting efforts to promote that detracts from the time you have to write. Time literally is money in this empowering new future, but having online marketing supports your digital sales. Many might think that simply having your book available for purchase online is enough and that money will roll in. For the average author, this simply isn't the case. You have to try things to see if they work for you.

Traditional houses are watching the self-published authors with solid sales and offering them contracts because they have a readership and a marketing platform that will come along with them. When I first sold, I had no idea how important my own marketing would become. Self-published authors today will know more than I did when I sold, but they will also have to weigh how important it will be for them to sell traditionally if it means giving up control of their copy rights and business decisions on pricing and other critical areas.

In my opinion, the number one best thing you can do—whether you get published traditionally or go the self-published route—is to write a good book. I can't stress this enough, so I am mentioning it here again. In either case, you'll need to build a readership, people who like what you do and will come back for more. Online promotion on various fronts is a good way to get the word out in a cost-effective manner to tap into a marketplace of the savvy readers we have today.

Ten Things I Believe About Writing—A Final Note

With all the uncertainty in our economy and in the publishing industry, in particular, I thought it might be important to talk about the passion to write. Passion to tell a story—our way—is the basic thing that drives authors with such conviction. Whether you read books or create them, novels can lift spirits, tug at imaginations, make us believe in the impossible, and take us for a journey into new worlds. (Talk about a cheap vacation!) Books dole out justice when it feels as if there's none and they transcend international borders, making this a small world after all.

If you're an aspiring author, I believe it's harder to get noticed by traditional publishers these days, yet with the digital boom in e-books, I feel there is even greater potential for getting discovered in a whole new way that still can feed your addiction to write and find an audience for your work. So take heart.

Below are my closing thoughts about writing and what I've learned on my journey.

1. **Tell YOUR story, your way.** If you have enough drive, you will discover a unique story that you *must* tell. If you're lucky, more stories will follow. Ideas for books can be a contagion worth embracing. If you use your life's experiences to filter through your characters, scenes and settings, only YOU can tell this story. How cool is that?

2. **Develop a tough skin.** There will always be negative people telling you that you can't write or reviewers who think you should quit. If it matters to you, you will learn from your mistakes and keep doing what's important to you. If anyone thinks writing a book is easy, let them try it.

3. **Be picky about what criticism you listen to.** Not every negative criticism will fit you. Too much "feedback" can dilute your voice or worm doubts into your head. Whatever your story, this is *your* book. You must have a sense of who you are as a writer in order to push back on any advice that doesn't fit you and only you can be the judge of that.

4. **Find the time to write regularly.** Even if it's only a few

hundred words or a page a day, set attainable goals but don't punish yourself if life gets in the way. Write because it matters to you, but don't make it another self-inflicted torture. Whether you get published or not, writing can add to your quality of life.

5. **Focus on the basics.** Writing is the only thing you can control. Selling your project, promoting it, dealing with proposals; these things are not in your hands and can become a mental road block. When things get tough, your writing is the backbone of your passion.

6. **Keep writing.** Don't wait by the phone or the mailbox while you have a proposal out. Get on to that next project and learn from your last one. Push the envelope of your craft, because you can. It's great to find success in a trend, but why not *be* the trend? Your breakout book or the one that gets you published could be your next idea.

7. **Trust your talent.** As human beings, we all have self-doubt. Some hide it better than others. We all deal with it, but the voice and talent you have shown with each new project will follow you. Trust your ability to tell a story, but also hone the craft of writing to be the best author you can be. Your basic talent will sustain you.

8. **Make the words bleed.** If the story is worth telling, it's usually because of the emotion you have to convey. Write what you fear, what you love, what you hate. Man has been telling stories since drawing on cave walls and within those stories has been the thrill of the hunt, the profound sorrow of death, or the joy of good fortune. Emotion connects us all, across any language barrier.

9. **Support other authors.** This is your world. Our world.

We're not in competition with each other. We're up against people who choose video games or movies over books. Make them see how powerful the written word can be, how it triggers the magic of our imaginations. Books are brain food. *READ* them! If you want to understand a genre, *READ IT!*

10. **Find a way to deal with rejections.** They will come, in one fashion or another, whether you're published or not. Create a ritual to dispel the negativity and move on, but if you don't risk rejection, you're not getting out there enough. Find a happy balance and keep writing. Not many feel passion for what they do. Count yourself lucky.

ONE AUTHOR'S AHA MOMENTS

Dedication

A very talented story teller—and amazing human being—helped me sell my first book and launched my writing career. This work is dedicated to New York Times and USA Today Bestselling author Sharon Sala. *I'm paying it forward, Sharon!*

Acknowledgements

There are countless individuals who have helped me in my writer's journey, from the authors who generously took time to put on conference workshops or to share their skill at monthly meetings, or those who take time from their writing to pass along their wisdom through blogging. One group blog has taught me many things and I'm privileged to be a contributing member at The Kill Zone (TKZ). I've learned so much from every member at TKZ and the many followers who share their own personal wisdom borne from the experience of writing. I'm also a contributing member of Adr3nalin3, a new dark YA group blog with amazing authors that started in Jan 2012. I'm looking forward to celebrating dark YA with them in the years to come.

I'd also like to thank those brave authors who have self-published books before me and gave me the courage to try it on my own. Authors James Scott Bell and the outspoken Joe Konrath are standouts in my mind.

I'm also always grateful for the support of my family and my husband, in particular. You have no idea how weird it is to live with

JORDAN DANE

an author, but my husband does it with style, grace, understanding, and his endearing humor.

ONE AUTHOR'S AHA MOMENTS

Praise for Jordan Dane

"Jordan Dane crafts nail-biting thrillers with guts and heart and a wicked sense of humor."
—*Jonathan Maberry, New York Times Bestseller*

"*In the Arms of Stone Angels* is eerie, dark and rich with unforgettable characters. A page turning suspense story that will haunt you long after you finish it. Jordan Dane is a fresh new voice in young adult paranormal fiction."
—*P. C. Cast, New York Times Bestseller*

"With a new take on the paranormal, Jordan Dane is one of the most compelling and honest voices in young adult fiction. Deliciously dark!"
—*Sophie Jordan, New York Times Bestseller*

"In her first YA novel, adult thriller writer Dane pens a macabre slow-burner, building tension by alternating Brenna's first-person narrative with sections in omniscient third; Brenna's peers, a deputy, and an observant doctor at White Bird's hospital all contribute insight into the mystery of Heather's death. Thoroughly eerie, the plot includes flashbacks and nightmares involving crossing over into the spirit world, while Dane's well-developed characters provide an authentic exploration of guilt, loyalty, and belonging."
—*Publishers Weekly for In the Arms of Stone Angels*

"Jordan Dane's *In the Arms of Stone Angels* is an unforgettable young

adult story that will leave you sleep deprived as you soon come to realize this is a new, fresh take on the paranormal. Dane has gone over the top to create a wonderful and suspenseful book that any teen will love. Each page brings new and exciting events that are completely unexpected."
—*Suspense Magazine*

"Dane's *On a Dark Wing* is a great new YA tale about death, love and starting over. It's an exciting mix that will remind readers of Bree Despain's *The Lost Saint* and Rachel Vincent's *Soul Screamers*. Paranormal fans will love this. A compelling page turner."
—*RT Magazine in a Featured Review*

Recognitions in Young Adult Fiction

In the Arms of Stone Angels made Bookyurt's Woot List for 2011. To earn that honor, according to Bookyurt, it has to amp Katie up, geek her out, and leave her ridiculously happy. Katie summed up by saying, "This book took me by storm. I didn't think any YA paranormal could surprise me at this stage, but did this book ever—and wow it packs quite a punch. I've already re-read it twice."

Jen at Fictitious Musings named *In the Arms of Stone Angels* and *On a Dark Wing* as "Most Deliciously Awesome Reads of 2011."

Emerging Novelists recognized *In the Arms of Stone Angels* as Winner of the Best Young Adult Novel of 2011.

Booktwirps named *In the Arms of Stone Angels* as Runner Up in the "Best of 2011" Paranormal.

www.ingramcontent.com/pod-product-compliance
Lightning Source LLC
Chambersburg PA
CBHW071317040426
42444CB00009B/2031